Social market or safety net?

British social rented housing in a European context

Mark Stephens, Nicky Burns and Lisa MacKay

The POLICY PRESS

First published in Great Britain in February 2002 by

The Policy Press
34 Tyndall's Park Road
Bristol BS8 1PY
UK

Tel no +44 (0)117 954 6800
Fax no +44 (0)117 973 7308
E-mail tpp@bristol.ac.uk
www.policypress.org.uk

© The Policy Press and the Joseph Rowntree Foundation 2002

Published for the Joseph Rowntree Foundation by The Policy Press

ISBN 1 86134 387 6

Mark Stephens is Senior Lecturer, **Nicky Burns** and **Lisa MacKay** were Research Assistants, all at the Department of Urban Studies, University of Glasgow. **Nicky Burns** is now a researcher in the Department of Geography and **Lisa MacKay** is studying in the Department of Social Policy and Social Work, University of Glasgow.

The **Joseph Rowntree Foundation** has supported this project as part of its programme of research and innovative development projects, which it hopes will be of value to policy makers, practitioners and service users. The facts presented and views expressed in this report are, however, those of the authors and not necessarily those of the Foundation.

The statements and opinions contained within this publication are solely those of the authors and contributors and not of The University of Bristol or The Policy Press. The University of Bristol and The Policy Press disclaim responsibility for any injury to persons or property resulting from any material published in this publication.

The Policy Press works to counter discrimination on grounds of gender, race, disability, age and sexuality.

Front cover: montage by Paul Durrant using image from PhotoDisc

Cover design by Qube Design Associates, Bristol
Printed in Great Britain by Hobbs the Printers Ltd, Southampton

Contents

Acknowledgements

This report relied on the active participation and support of many people.

We would like to thank the country experts who completed the questionnaire, responded to queries and commented on drafts. They were in alphabetical order of country: Jens Lunde (Denmark), Sirpa Tulla and Keijo Tanner (Finland), Didier Cornuel (France), Horst Tomann (Germany), Peter Boelhouwer (the Netherlands), Ian MacArthur and Bengt Turner (Sweden).

Questionnaires were followed up by country visits to Denmark, Finland, the Netherlands and Sweden in September 2000. We would like to thank Harri Hiltunen, Ian MacArthur, Hugo Priemus and Hedvig Vestigaard for providing introductions and helping to arrange interviews. We would also like to thank those people whom we met or interviewed:

Denmark: Boligselskabernes Landsforening: Keld Adsbøl and Steffen Boel Jørgensen; Boligkontoret: Michael Demsitz; Copenhagen Business School: Jens Lunde; Danish Building and Research Institute (SBI): Hedvig Vestergaard and Hans Skifter Andersen.

Finland: ARA: Harri Hiltunen, Ari Laine and Tero Tuomisto; Environment Ministry: Keijo Tanner, Kari Matikainen and Timo Tähtinen; Espoonkruunu Oy: Esa Eichhorn, Kirsi Mäkinen and colleagues; Finance Ministry: Sirpa Tulla.

The Netherlands: AEDES: Erik Wilke; CBP: Jacco Hakfoort; Genuagroep: R. Rotscheid and R. Franchimont; OTB: Hugo Priemus and Peter Boelhouwer; WSW: Roland van der Post and Sybro Bruinsma.

Sweden: Government Inquiry on Non-profit Housing: Per Åhrén and Ian McArthur; SABO: Jonas Schneider and Lars Sundqvist; SBAB: Lars Berstig; Svenska Bostäder: Gilles Edholm, Carl-Erik Augustsson, Mats Rosborg and colleagues.

We are especially grateful for the time and effort of staff at Svenska Bostäder (Stockholm) and Espoonkruunu Oy (Espoo) for organising visits to see housing under their management, and for their hospitality.

David Fenton (Ernst & Young), Barbara Alinger (The Housing Finance Corporation), Steve Wilcox (University of York), Mark Lupton (Chartered Institute of Housing) and our colleagues, Suzanne Fitzpatrick, Peter Kemp and Alison More, all provided invaluable information and advice. Useful feedback was given by David Donnison and other participants in a Department of Urban Studies seminar in February 2001.

Jeane Jenkins provided vital secretarial support.

All projects depend on the time and cooperation of their advisory committee: Stephen Duckworth (National Housing Federation), Raymond Kershaw (Department of the Environment, Transport and the Regions/Department for Transport, Local Government and the Regions), Duncan Maclennan (Scottish Executive), Hugo Priemus (OTB Research Institute for Housing, Urban and Mobility Studies, Delft University of Technology), Andrew Parfitt (Department for Transport, Local Government and the Regions), John Perry (Chartered Institute of Housing), Sue Regan (Institute of Public Policy Research) and Christine Whitehead (London School of Economics).

Finally we are grateful to Michael Sturge, who managed the project at the Joseph Rowntree Foundation and chaired the advisory committee. In particular we thank him for his patience and support as the project was delayed by Mark Stephens' broken leg.

Of course responsibility for errors of fact or interpretation remain the responsibility of the authors.

Mark Stephens, Nicky Burns and Lisa MacKay
Glasgow, October 2001

Summary

In most northern European countries, social rented sectors were developed in the decades following 1945. However, different institutional structures and funding mechanisms were adopted to meet this common end. Moreover, secondary objectives of the sector also diverged between safety net and wider affordability objectives. This report provides a practical examination of the social rented sector in Britain and in six other European countries: Denmark, France, Finland, Germany, the Netherlands and Sweden. The principal purpose of the study is to inform the development of housing policy in Britain.

The role of the social rented sector

In the decades following the war, governments in northern Europe generally developed social rented sectors. A common motivation was to alleviate housing shortages. In four of the countries surveyed, including Britain, the social rented sector now makes up around 20% of the housing stock. The Netherlands has the largest social rented sector (more than 33%), and Germany the smallest (6%).

There is no consistent trend in the size of the social rented sector. While it has diminished greatly in Britain and Germany as a result of government policy, it has exhibited stability elsewhere. Production fell generally in the 1990s, usually due to financial constraints, but Britain had the smallest social housing building programme.

As the importance of social rented housing in meeting housing shortages has diminished, differences in its role have emerged. Britain places much importance on using the social rented sector as a safety net for vulnerable households, and is the only country where there exists a legally enforceable right to housing for specified groups. Various mechanisms exist in other countries to ensure that social rented housing provides a safety net function, for example through the use of local authority nominations in Denmark and Sweden. But in France, social landlords are often reluctant to house the poorest households.

The social rented sector in other countries performs a greater role in enhancing housing affordability for a wider range of income groups than is the case in Britain. Income limits exist in Finland, France and Germany, but these are sufficiently high as to permit income mixing. Allocation procedures often depart from the needs-based system commonly operated in Britain. Priority is given to existing tenants of estates in Denmark while application-driven systems, where time waited is the main 'currency', are widely used in the Netherlands.

British housing exhibits a greater level of inter-tenure polarisation than in the other countries studied. After adjusting for the relative size of the social rented sector, households from the poorest two income deciles are much more likely to be housed in the sector than in the other countries. Moreover, the rate at which the use of the sector falls as incomes rise is most dramatic in Britain. Thus social rented housing is distributed as if it were a strictly means-tested benefit in Britain, as if it were a less severely means-tested benefit in the Netherlands and Germany, and as if it were a flat-rate benefit with a relatively high upper income limit in France. It is notable that this pattern is not the result of the exclusion of nuclear families from the British social rented sector – in common with France and Germany there is a greater proportion of nuclear families in the British social rented sector than in the population as a whole. Further analysis showed that greater income inequality in Britain combines with tenure polarisation to give British social renters substantially lower average incomes compared to the national average than their counterparts in the other countries.

The provision of social rented housing

The study showed that Britain has been unusual in providing social rented housing which has been owned and managed by local government on a (near) monopoly basis. As Britain moves away from this model, this study indicated that four main types of social landlord were used in the other countries studied. Municipal housing companies, which enjoy greater operational autonomy than British local authority housing departments, are the main providers of social rented housing in Sweden, Finland and Germany, while a weaker form of municipal housing company provides the bulk of French social rented housing. Housing associations are the preferred model in Denmark and the Netherlands, while a variety of non- (or limited) profit companies operate in France, Finland and Germany. Germany is unusual in providing much social rented housing through private sector landlords. A major cause of the shrinking of the German social rented sector is this housing passing into the market rented sector once subsidised loans have been repaid. Outside Britain local monopolies seldom exist.

Social landlords are generally bound by rules relating to registration, regulation of activities, auditing and supervision. There was a general deregulation of the social rented sector in the Netherlands and Germany in the 1980s and 1990s. However, the most recent policy proposals of the Netherlands government indicate an effort to regain some leverage over the operation of housing associations, limiting their diversification into commercial property development, but also encouraging a widening of their social objectives.

Financial organisations linked with the social rented sector often play a regulatory role – for example the state funding body in France, the state housing fund in Finland and the guarantee fund in the Netherlands. In countries where

dependence on private finance has increased, the importance of external agencies in monitoring social landlords' financial and managerial profile has risen.

Rent setting

While rent setting at below market rents is a key feature of social rented housing, recent policy debate in Britain has focused on anomalies in rent structures between regions, landlords in the same region and within landlords. In the countries studied, rent setting at the level of the landlord is determined by the debt structure of the organisation, subject to various subsidies that are generally designed to tackle the 'front-end loading' problem that makes debt most expensive to serve in its earliest years. In Britain a distinct advantage of monopoly local landlords has been the ability to pool rents, limiting rent anomalies between old and new properties. The more fragmented structure of the social rented sector in some of the other countries studied limits the opportunity to pool rents, although it is now permitted in Germany and actively encouraged in Finland. Denmark's cost rental system operates largely at an estate level and this creates particularly acute rent anomalies with older, popular properties in central areas sometimes having lower rents than newer, peripheral and less popular estates. Other countries, including the Netherlands and Sweden, also reported anomalies in rents at the level of the landlord, with rent structures often failing to reflect fully differentials in popularity.

The report established that rent rises in the 1990s had been greatest in Britain, Finland and Sweden. These countries recorded real rent increases of more than 30%. In Sweden rent rises are agreed in negotiations between local landlords and tenants' associations. The French government issues guidelines, but landlords are free to set rents as they wish, while cost rental principles apply in Germany, Finland and Denmark (subject to small profits in Germany and Finland). In recent years the British government has introduced more central control over rent increases in England, a policy also followed by the Dutch government. It was noted that credit rating agencies have expressed concern that such rent controls limit the financial flexibility of landlords and might endanger long-term maintenance.

Housing allowances

Several features of the British Housing Benefit system have attracted criticism. There are three main complaints: first, that recipients of social assistance do not have to make a contribution to their rent; second, that all recipients are insulated entirely from rent rises; and third, that the steep taper (the determinant of the rate of benefit withdrawal as incomes rise) creates a poverty trap.

This study indicated that these features are unusual, but the distinctive nature of the British system is attributable to its function as a safety net, designed to prevent post-rent incomes falling below social assistance levels. Moreover, British social assistance payments do not make any provision for housing costs.

Housing allowance schemes in the other countries fall into two further categories. First, in Sweden, Finland and Denmark the housing allowance system fulfils an affordability function, whereas a safety net is provided by the social assistance system. Eligibility for housing allowance must be tested before social assistance. Second, in the Netherlands, the housing allowance also performs primarily an affordability function, but since social assistance provides only standard allowances for housing costs, it is possible for post-rent incomes to fall below social assistance levels. Germany operates a system that is similar to the Dutch system, except that additional payments from social assistance may be made if post-rent incomes fall too far. While the systems operated in other countries do not pay all a tenant's rent, they are also withdrawn less quickly as incomes rise.

While there is no common trend in the numbers of housing allowance claimants in the 1990s, real costs were higher at the end of the period in all countries where figures are available. Sweden was the only country to have achieved significant reductions in housing allowance costs. These had almost returned to their 1990 levels by 1999. The savings were achieved in part by falling unemployment, but also by excluding childless claimants aged 29-65 from the system. Such

households can seek protection from social assistance.

The study indicated that a higher proportion (almost 66%) of British social tenants are dependent on housing allowances than in the other countries – one third in the Netherlands and Sweden, around 40% in Finland and 50% in France. The high (60%) proportion of Danish social tenants receiving housing allowances is attributable to a generous scheme operated for pensioners. The study also found that Britain devotes a higher proportion of GDP to housing allowances than the other countries.

Further analysis revealed that the high level of housing allowance dependence and expenditure in Britain is attributable to inter-tenure polarisation, greater labour market polarisation and the lack of generosity of the social security system.

Financing social rented housing: subsidies and surpluses

Housing subsidies are usually designed to reduce the level or the cost of servicing housing debt in its early years when its real burden is greatest. The need for such subsidies has diminished as inflation and interest rates have converged downwards throughout the advanced economies. Pressures on government budgets have also increased, although there is evidence that many European governments experienced falling debt as a result of lower interest rates and falling unemployment, rather than by reducing underlying subsidy commitments. Expenditure may be squeezed during a future recession.

A variety of subsidy instruments are operated by the countries surveyed. State loans are still a feature of the French and Finnish systems, whereas Britain relies much more heavily on capital grants (in the housing association sector) than any other country. Recurrent subsidies are mainly a feature of the German system and British local authorities. The most common form of subsidy is the interest rate subsidy, which is often reduced over time. The Netherlands has now abolished subsidies, having first provided the housing associations with payments designed to relieve them of debt. Sweden's interest rate subsidy system has now been replaced with the equivalent of a tax allowance (for new loans).

The research showed that as many social rented systems move towards surplus, these surpluses are sometimes captured in part by government (Sweden and Britain), or redistributed between landlords through mergers (the Netherlands and Britain). Denmark provides an example of a transparent mechanism for redistributing surpluses between landlords through a sector-wide building fund.

Private finance

Private finance is of major importance in promoting social rented housing in all the countries surveyed other than France. It is usually sourced from the dominant types of financial intermediary in each country. Special intermediaries exist in Britain and the Netherlands to help access capital markets on behalf of social landlords. British social landlords are unusual in accessing the capital markets directly. The most extensive securitisation programme exists in Finland, whereby state loans are securitised in order to provide funding for new loans or interest subsidies.

The survey suggested that the cost of private finance tends to be higher in Britain than in the other countries. The measurement of the cost of funding is extremely complex and this finding requires more detailed investigation. However, a likely explanatory factor is the absence of a loan guarantee system in Britain.

Conclusions and recommendations

Three main conclusions were reached:

1. British social housing operates in a different social and economic context from the other countries studied. Britain experiences higher levels of inequality and poverty and, consequently, the social rented sector provides a safety net for vulnerable households in Britain. Its role in enhancing housing affordability for a wider range of income groups is evident in the other countries.

2. The priority given to the social rented sector of providing a safety net makes it difficult to create a social market within it. Tenants in British social rented housing are very poor and it is very difficult for them to exercise market or market-type choices. Where they do, they are likely to do so from a weak position in relation to others.

3. Consequently, the priority in British housing policy should be to ensure that the social rented sector provides a comprehensive and high quality safety net.

Ten more specific recommendations were drawn from these conclusions:

1. The social rented sector should be governed by broad objectives established by government. These should be wide enough to command widespread political consensus. While the sector should be regulated and accountable, it should be insulated from short-term political interference to encourage long-term planning, particularly relating to maintenance.

2. Allocations policy should be directed at providing housing for homeless and other vulnerable groups. Allocations systems should be designed to ensure that they do not weaken the choices of the most vulnerable applicants.

3. Social rented housing should be provided by a variety of institutional types, and local monopolies avoided.

4. Two types of social landlord should be avoided. First, private landlords, because they are better suited as vehicles for removing housing shortages, rather than tackling enduring affordability problems and safety net priorities. Second, local authorities, which sit uneasily beside the need to create a culture of long-term planning into British rented housing.

5. Social landlords should operate within a common legal, financial and regulatory regime. This framework should aim to encourage solidarity within the sector.

6. A rent surplus fund for the entire social rented sector should be established. Funds should be used to (i) facilitate common rent policies, (ii) provide funds for long-term maintenance in financially weak landlords, and (iii) provide funds for development.

7. Rent rises should be agreed annually by representatives of the surplus fund, the sector and tenants. Some direction over funds would be necessary to ensure that fair contributions are made to the surplus fund.

8. Housing Benefit should continue to meet the entire housing costs of tenants living in social rented housing who are in receipt of social assistance.

9. The case for a guarantee fund based on the Dutch model should be considered. A detailed study into the cost of private finance in Britain is required.

10. Policy should be reviewed in (say) ten years' time. It is possible that labour market and social security reforms will have created more favourable conditions for the broadening of the function of the social rented sector.

Introduction

In the decades following the Second World War, most countries in northern Europe developed social rented sectors. Initially, all served the purpose of alleviating housing shortages. But the way in which social rented housing was financed, and the agencies chosen to develop and manage it varied. Moreover, the function of the social rented sector began to diverge as general housing shortages disappeared.

This report provides a practical examination of the social rented sector in Britain and in six other European countries: Denmark, France, Finland, Germany, the Netherlands and Sweden. These countries were selected because the social rented sector played an important role in each of them. The principal purpose of the study is to inform the development of housing policy in Britain, although it is hoped that it will be of interest to readers in other countries.

Of course housing policy differs in different parts of the United Kingdom. In tables and figures we have been careful to specify the territory to which British data refer. When different data or policies are evident, we have distinguished between England and Scotland, but we have not attempted to describe the housing system in Wales or Northern Ireland. In the text we have often used the deliberately vague term 'Britain' when generalisations can be made about different parts of Great Britain. Occasionally, it was necessary to distinguish between the current united Germany and the former West and East Germany.

We considered it very important to consider housing policy within the social and economic context in which it is developed, and in Chapter 2 we use this to aid understanding of the role which the social rented sector plays in different countries. In Chapter 3 an overview is given of the different types of landlord who provide social rented housing. Chapters 4 and 5 deal with the pricing of social rented housing: rent setting and housing allowances respectively. Chapters 6 and 7 deal with housing finance: subsidy systems and private finance. In Chapter 8 conclusions are drawn and recommendations made.

The study was conducted in four stages. First, a questionnaire was completed by country experts in six of the countries surveyed (with equivalent information collected for Britain by the research team). Second, the research team visited Denmark, Finland, the Netherlands and Sweden to discuss issues in more depth with representatives of the social rented sector, social landlords, policy experts and organisations dealing with housing finance. Third, a draft report was circulated around country experts, the advisory committee and some of the interviewees for comment. The final report was then drafted.

2

The role of the social rented sector

Introduction

There is no simple definition of social rented housing that fits every country equally well. For example, it is usually, but not always, provided by not for profit organisations. The European Liaison Committee for Social Housing (CECODHAS) has adopted the following definition: 'rental ... housing for which access rules are defined in favouring households that have difficulties in finding accommodation'.

Social rented housing has traditionally fulfilled four functions. These are to:

- reduce shortages of housing;
- improve the affordability of housing;
- allow people to gain access to adequate housing who could not afford to do so in the free market; and
- act as a safety net for more marginal households who would otherwise be homeless.

While these categories overlap, the extent to which each of these objectives is pursued varies between countries and so shapes the character of the social rented sector. Consequently, the role that it fulfils within the housing system can vary greatly. This, in turn, influences other policies such as allocation and pricing, and the extent to which a policy might be transferred successfully from one country to another.

This chapter aims to identify the role that the social rented sector does play within the wider housing system. This is tackled in four ways:

1. Contextual information tracing the size and trends in the size of the social rented sector since 1980 is provided.

2. Levels of new building in the social rented sector are presented to indicate the extent to which the sector is being promoted to meet housing shortages.
3. The allocation policies and systems are examined to determine the target groups for the social rented sector at entry.
4. The distribution of income groups and household types in each tenure is examined to determine the extent to which each social rented sector focuses on the task of housing the poorest households.

Trends in the size of the social rented sector

The most recent data on the composition of tenure (Table 1) indicate that:

- In four of the seven countries examined, the social rented sector represents around one fifth of the housing stock[1]. The outliers are the Netherlands, whose social rented sector forms more than one third of the housing stock and Germany where the social rented sector forms less than 6% of the stock.
- The similarity in size of the social rented sector in four of the countries is accompanied by disparities in the size of the other tenures. Among these countries Great Britain and Finland have by far the highest levels of owner occupation (at around two thirds of the stock), while half the housing stock in Germany is privately rented – by far the highest proportion among the countries surveyed.

[1] Note the much larger scale of social renting in Scotland compared to the British average. In Scotland, the social rented sector still forms about 30% of the housing stock, some 10 percentage points higher than in Great Britain.

Table 1: Housing tenure (%)

Year	c. 1980	c. 1990	c. 2000
Denmark	1980[a]	1991[b]	1999[c]
(a) Owner	52.0	58.1	55.3
(b) Social rent		20.9	19.3
(c) Private rent	41.0	16.3	18.3
(d) Co-op	8.0	4.7	–
Finland	1980	1990[d]	1997[f]
(a) Owner	61.0[d]	67.0	66.1
(b) Social rent	12.5[e]	15.0	16.0
(c) Private rent	9.6[e]	9.0	14.7
(d) Other	–	–	3.2
France	1984[g]	1988[g]	1997[h]
(a) Owner	51.2	54.3	54.4
(b) Social rent	16.2	17.1	19.6
(c) Private rent	22.2	19.7	23.9
(d) Other	–	9.0	1.9
West Germany	1978[j]	1987[j]	1994[k]
(a) Owner	38.0	38.0	42.0
(b) Social rent	18.0	15.0	10.0
(c) Private rent	45.0	43.0	48.0
(d) Co-op	–	4.0	–
Germany			1998[k]
(a) Owner	–	–	43.8
(b) Social rent	–	–	5.6
(c) Private rent	–	–	50.6
Netherlands	1980[l]	1990[l]	1998[m]
(a) Owner	42.0	45.0	50.8
(b) Social rent	34.0	36.0	35.6
(c) Private rent	24.0	17.0	11.3
Sweden	1980[n]	1990[n]	
(a) Owner	42.0	43.0	–
(b) Social rent	23.0	23.0	–
(c) Private rent	19.0	17.0	–
(d) Co-op	16.0	16.0	–
Great Britain[p]	1981	1990	1998
(a) Owner	55.8	65.8	67.6
(b) Social rent	33.0	25.0	21.9
(c) Private rent	11.2	9.2	10.6
England[p]	1981	1990	1998
(a) Owner	57.7	67.1	68.0
(b) Social rent	30.9	23.2	20.9
(c) Private rent	11.4	9.7	11.1
Scotland[p]	1981	1990	1998
(a) Owner	35.6	51.2	61.3
(b) Social rent	54.3	42.9	31.9
(c) Private rent	11.8	6.0	6.7

Sources:
[a] European Commission (1993) *Statistics on Housing in the EC*, p 60; [b] Power (1993), Table 25.3; [c] country expert; [d] Doling (1997), Tables 9.1, 10.1, 11.1; [e] Ministry of the Environment (1997) *Housing Indicators*; [f] country expert; [g] Oxley & Smith (1996), Table 8.1; [h] country expert; [j] McCrone & Stephens (1995), Table 4.1; [k] country expert; [l] McCrone & Stephens (1995), Table 5.2; [m] country expert; [n] McCrone & Stephens (1995), Table 7.1; [p] DoE/DETR *Housing and construction statistics*, various issues

An analysis of tenure trends since 1980 indicates that:

- There is no consistent trend in the size of the social rented sector. In Denmark, Finland, France, the Netherlands and Sweden (up to 1990) the social rented sector has exhibited stability or slow growth. Yet in West Germany and Great Britain the social rented sector has shrunk by perhaps one third over the period. In Scotland the fall has been even greater (more than 40%), albeit from a much higher base.
- There is no evidence of an inexorable rise of home ownership. Three of the countries (Denmark, Finland and France) register modest increases in owner occupation over the past two decades, but there have been falls since 1990 in Denmark and Finland. The Netherlands and West Germany have experienced a more sustained growth in owner occupation, but Britain is outstanding in raising the home owner rate by 12 percentage points since 1980. The rise of home ownership in Scotland is still more dramatic: a 25 percentage point increase since 1980 has taken Scotland's home owner rate from the lowest level of any of the countries surveyed in 1980 to a level higher than any non-British country other than Finland.

In summary, there is little evidence to suggest that a convergence of housing systems in terms of tenure is occurring. When the dramatic tenure changes that have arisen in Britain and West Germany are set aside, the remaining picture is one of relative stability.

Indeed, the notable shrinkage of the social rented sectors in Britain and Germany are attributable to particular policies so cannot be attributed to common external forces:

- In Germany the reduction in the size of the social rented sector arises from social rented houses owned by for-profit landlords passing into the private rented sector once subsidised loans are repaid. The decline of the social rented sector in Germany as a consequence of subsidy design reflects the relatively high importance attached to social rented housing's role in meeting housing shortages in relation to other objectives.

Table 2: Social rented housing construction[a] 1990–98

	Denmark	France	Finland	Germany	NL	Sweden	UK
1990	2.1	0.8	3.4	1.1	1.9	1.6	0.6
1991	1.8	1.0	3.2	1.2	1.5	1.7	0.6
1992	1.3	1.1	2.9	1.4	1.6	1.7	0.6
1993	1.2	1.3	3.4	1.9	1.5	1.1	0.7
1994	1.1	1.3	2.0	2.0	1.6	0.7	0.7
1995	0.9	1.1	2.1	1.8	1.6	0.4	0.7
1996	0.7	0.9	2.6	1.5	1.7	0.3	0.6
1997	1.1	0.9	2.1	1.3	1.3	0.3	0.5
1998	0.9	0.8	1.6	1.0	1.0	0.2	0.4[b]
Average[c]	**1.2**	**1.0**	**2.6**	**1.5**	**1.5**	**0.9**	**0.6**

Notes:
[a] per 1,000 population
[b] Great Britain only
[c] sum of columns/9 (years)
Source: Authors' calculations based on country experts; UK = Wilcox (2000)

- In Britain, much of the fall in the size of the social rented sector has been caused by the Right to Buy (RTB) which, of course, also has the effect of raising the level of owner occupation[2]. This reflects the shift in the objectives of housing policy, away from using social rented housing to accommodate a broader section of society and towards providing a safety net.

Meeting housing shortages

In the post-war period social rented housing was commonly used to reduce housing shortages. Table 2 indicates that during the 1990–98 period, the role of the social rented sector in meeting housing shortages was generally scaled down. Nevertheless there are important variations:

- Britain had the smallest building programme in the social rented sector. Britain built fewer social rented homes per capita for four

---

[2] Around two million dwellings have been sold under RTB, accounting for about 8% of the housing stock or 12% of the stock of owner occupied dwellings. If these former social rented dwellings are subtracted from the current stock of owner occupied dwellings, the sector shrinks to 59.5%. Over the period the owner occupied sector [including RTB] rose from 55.8% of the total to 67.5%. RTB was responsible for around 68% of the increase in the percentage share of owner occupation (authors' calculations, based on *Housing and construction statistics*, DoE/DETR, various issues).

consecutive years, equalled the lowest level in the fifth year, and had the second lowest level of construction for the remaining three years of the period.
- Finland had by far the highest level of output. This partly arises from the decision to maintain subsidised production during the recession.
- No country was producing more social rented houses per capita at the end of the period than they were at its beginning.
- We can distinguish between countries where production at first rose and then fell (Germany and France), those where it more or less consistently fell (Denmark, Finland, and the Netherlands), Sweden where production collapsed in the mid-1990s, and Britain where it fell gently from a consistently low base.

The decline in social rented housing production has a variety of causes, including:

- *Direct financial burden:* In Denmark, the municipalities' contribution towards the costs of social rented housing has been increased, and has resulted in a reluctance to sanction new building.
- *Indirect financial burden:* In Finland, Denmark and Germany, where local government bears a considerable share of the cost of providing services, some local authorities are reluctant to build housing for low income groups, fearing that they will increase the demand for local services while not contributing significantly to the local tax base.

- *Cost limits:* In Sweden, limits set by central government reduce the share of construction costs eligible for subsidy to the extent that social landlords are reluctant to build, even when demand is high.
- *Lack of demand:* In the Netherlands, social landlords cite lack of demand, rather than changes in finance, as the main reason for the reduction in the development programme since the mid-1990s.
- *Planning system:* The Dutch government has agreed to concentrate new housebuilding on certain high-growth areas, known as VINEX locations. Under these arrangements, social rented housing is restricted to 30% of the total.
- *Housing boom:* The boom in the owner occupied sector is sometimes cited as a cause of reduced levels of social rented housing construction. In Finland, developers' enthusiasm for building social rented housing has diminished now that the owner occupied sector offers higher profits, while social landlords in Sweden have difficulty in bidding against the private sector to acquire building land. (Land allocation by competitive bidding is a new feature of the Swedish system. Previously land was allocated by local government.)

Of course the crude figures do not tell us the extent to which housing shortages exist. But they do indicate that the ability of social rented housing to meet regional shortages has generally diminished.

Affordability, need and safety net: the allocation of social rented housing

Possibly the key characteristic of social rented housing is that its entry point is determined by administrative processes, rather than price rationing. In Britain, local authorities have been left free to devise their own allocation policies, within broad and largely unenforceable guidelines. The crucial exception to this lies in the legislation under which local authorities are obliged to house priority categories of unintentionally homeless people. This constitutes a legally enforceable right to housing. Over time local authority waiting lists have tended to shift towards emphasising housing need over other criteria, an approach mirrored by the policies of the Housing Corporation and Scottish Homes

(Fitzpatrick and Stephens, 1999). (However, Pawson and Kintrea [2002] note that the vast majority of local authorities in Scotland and England continue to take account of waiting time when prioritising applications. In areas of chronic low demand, the notion of rationing has become redundant, causing needs-based systems to be reassessed.) Thus in Britain the role of social housing in providing a safety net is well established.

In the countries studied, central governments do not operate strict allocation rules over social landlords, and there is no equivalent of the British homelessness legislation. Despite the existence of income limits at the point of entry in Finland, France and Germany, these are set sufficiently high to permit income mixing. Following concerns that social landlords in France were avoiding housing the most needy, the Loi Besson, passed in 1990, introduced a quasi-constitutional right to housing. In practice this has amounted to greater inter-agency cooperation at county and local levels to match better housing supply with housing needs, while additional subsidies have been introduced to encourage social landlords to provide more housing for the most disadvantaged, something that they remain reluctant to do (Blanc, 1998).

In the Netherlands and Finland, social landlords are required by law to cater for disadvantaged groups. The Dutch law, consolidated in 1993, which sets social landlords five broad performance targets, requires social landlords to give preference to a target group consisting of people with incomes below a modal point (Walker, 1998). Although this income point has been uprated by inflation and the numbers of eligible households remain stable, the proportion of households included has fallen from 50% in the mid-1980s to just under 40% now – still a very broad section of society (Remkes, 2000). In practice, local authorities and social landlords are left to devise their own allocation policies within the broad framework set by central government.

Traditionally, a needs-based waiting list system similar to that operated in Britain was used in the Netherlands, but in the 1990s about one third of local authorities covering half the social rented sector adopted application-driven systems, commonly (and misleadingly) named 'choice'-based models. These have attracted much interest in England, where the DTLR is currently funding 27 pilot schemes (DETR, 2000a). Within Scotland, Edinburgh City Council is implementing an application-driven pilot. Under the Dutch systems, properties are advertised in free newspapers and households are free to apply for them. Allocations are made on the basis of applicants' points which are notified in advance. Points are awarded on a time-basis: length of tenancy for existing tenants and age for others. Two other restrictions come into play: first, the household size must be appropriate for the dwelling and, second, the household should be able to afford the rent. A parallel needs-based system is usually operated to cater for urgent cases. These usually amount to 10–20% of total allocations, a much lower proportion than allocations to homeless households in some parts of Britain. The objective of the system is to try to introduce choice into the allocation process, as in the market sector, but with points replacing money as the currency.

Application-driven systems have not always fulfilled the objectives of their creators. For example, some people make blanket applications for dwellings and consequently there remains a high rejection rate. But the key point is that choice-based systems cannot escape *any* of the trade-offs that exist within traditional needs-based waiting lists. Much of the discussion surrounding application-driven allocations in Britain confuses the *currency* used under the Dutch choice-based systems and the *method* of application[3]. The method of allocation of necessity changes when waiting lists are dropped in favour of the application-driven model. But the outcome is still likely to depend on whether the *currency* is also changed, that is, whether it is time-based or needs-based. Applicants exercise *constrained* choices within both waiting list and application-based systems. But the extent to which choices are constrained is determined primarily by the *currency* adopted rather than the method of application.

When time-based systems are adopted, as is commonly the case in the Netherlands, most explicit and implicit choice is given to applicants in least need, since they are able to refuse offers with impunity (Kullberg, 1997). This has been a feature of many British allocation systems and has

been blamed for leading to the most disadvantaged households being housed in the least desirable accommodation (Fitzpatrick and Stephens, 1999). There are strong similarities between the practice, often used in waiting lists, of limiting the number of offers that homeless households can reject compared to general needs applicants, and the creation of 'a time limited "priority card"' for needy households under some of the DTLR pilots (DETR, 2001a, p 3). Similarly, there is little practical difference between a household rejecting an offer under a waiting list system and simply not applying under an application-led system.

As has been noted, the safety net role played by the British social rented sector is explicitly recognised by law, and is demonstrated by the high proportion of lettings to homeless households. That the Dutch system caters for a much broader section of society (to be discussed later) does not seem to have been given much consideration in relation to this piece of policy transfer. (It is, however, difficult to think of objections to application-based allocations for hard to let housing.)

The Finnish system of income mixing is possible because Finnish social rented housing plays less of a safety net function than is the case in Britain. Social landlords are required by law to ensure that state subsidies are channelled towards socio-economically disadvantaged residents on a means-tested basis. In reality, the local authorities seem to interpret the law liberally, and pursue policies of income mixing. For example, Espoo, a large local authority within the Helsinki metropolitan area operates a strict income mixing policy in order to avoid segregation, even though this means not always housing the neediest households.

In Denmark and Sweden, social landlords are able to operate their own allocation systems, subject to local authority quotas. These are set at 25% in Denmark, and are used mainly to house recipients of social assistance (OECD, 1999). Allocations outside the quota system are made according to a strict hierarchy – residents of the estate come first, tenants of the social landlord living outside the estate come second, and applicants from outside the housing association come last. Swedish local authorities are able to set their own quotas. In Stockholm, one third of all allocations are made by the local authority.

---

[3] Self-evidently choice-based models do not 'scrap' bureaucracy, as was claimed by the DETR (2001a, p 3). They merely change the bureaucratic process.

Thereafter, landlords are able to devise their own allocation criteria. For example, Svenska Bostäder, the largest municipal housing company in Stockholm, gives priority to sons and daughters of their tenants.

Who lives in the social rented sector?

Income groups

While the allocation policies of social landlords determines the flow of tenants into social rented housing, it tells us little about the population of social tenants as a whole. To gain a full picture of the role of the social rented sector, we conducted an analysis of the composition of the three main tenures by income group. Data was available for the Netherlands, France, Great Britain and Germany.

Figure 1 indicates the distribution of households from each income decile throughout the three tenures, adjusting for the different tenure pattern in each country. For example, there is literally more room for more people from across the income range to live in the large Dutch social rented sector. The distribution is standardised by dividing the proportion of each income decile living in social rented housing by the size of that sector. If households were evenly distributed between tenures then the expected result would be 1. If there is a disproportionate number of households from a particular income decile in a particular tenure, then the result will be greater than 1. Conversely, if there are fewer than expected, then the result will be less than 1.

Figure 1a shows that:

- Households from the bottom two income deciles are much more likely to be housed in the social rented sector in Britain than is the case in France, the Netherlands and Germany.
- Poorer households in the Netherlands and Germany are also more likely to be housed in the social rented sector, but the concentration of the very poorest households is not as high as in Britain, and the rate at which representation falls as incomes rise is more gradual than is the case in Britain.
- The French social rented sector houses the broadest range of households from across the income spectrum, compared to Britain, Germany and the Netherlands

In summary, social rented housing appears to be distributed as if it were a strictly means-tested benefit in Britain; as if it were a less severely means-tested benefit in the Netherlands and Germany; and as if it were a flat-rate benefit with a relatively high upper income limit in France.

An analysis of the distribution of income groups in the other tenures (Figures 1b and 1c) reveals that:

- The private rented sector also caters disproportionately for very low income households, particularly in France and Britain. However, high income groups also use this tenure.
- The distribution of income groups in the privately rented sector is much more even in the Netherlands and Germany, than in France and Britain. This is caused principally by lower levels of usage among very low income households, rather than higher usage by middle and high income groups.
- The relative use of the owner occupied sector among income groups is much more similar between countries than is the case with the other tenures.
- Despite RTB, there are fewer owner occupiers in the lowest decile than one would expect given the size of the tenure in Britain compared to the other countries.

Ages and household types

It is possible that Britain's social rented sector houses such a high concentration of low income households merely because it is likely to house certain types of households. Moreover, if nuclear families are greatly underrepresented in British social rented housing, the 'equivalent' incomes of social tenants (that is, incomes adjusted for the size and composition of households) might actually be higher than is suggested by the preceding analysis.

Figure 1a: Representation of income groups in the social rented sector

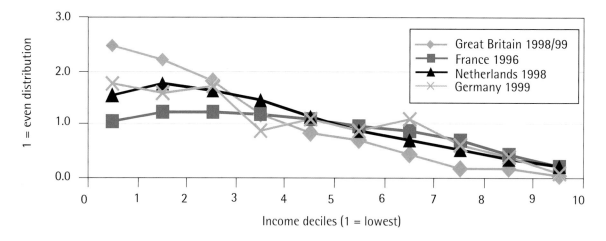

Source: Country experts; GB source = Family Spending

Figure 1b: Representation of income groups in the private rented sector

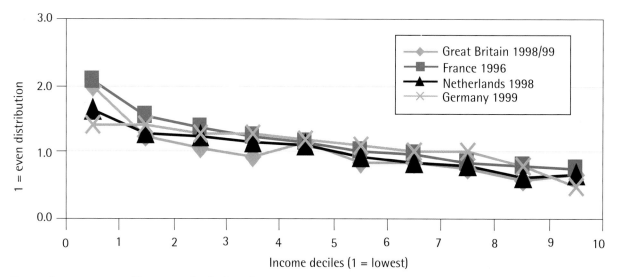

Source: Country experts; GB source = Family Spending

Figure 1c: Representation of income groups in the owner-occupied sector

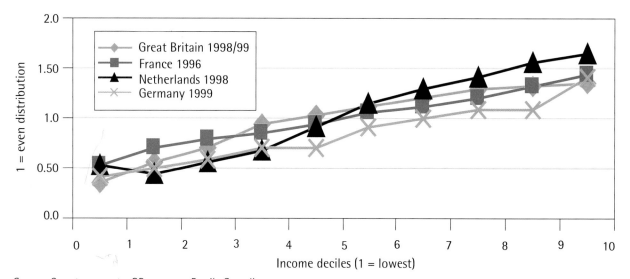

Source: Country experts; GB source = Family Spending

Figure 2a displays the distribution of age groups in the social rented sectors in the Netherlands, Great Britain and Germany. France's distribution appears in a separate graph as the age categorisations are somewhat different (Figure 2b). Figure 2a indicates that:

- The social rented sectors in Britain, the Netherlands and Germany display a similar age distribution, with an overrepresentation of young households, an underrepresentation of intermediate age groups and, in the case of the Netherlands and Britain, an overrepresentation of retired households.

- Britain has the highest concentration of young households, given the size of the tenure, but the preponderance of older households to occupy the sector is no greater than in the Netherlands.

- France's social rented sector has an unusual age structure, with the use of the sector peaking in the 30–39 age group before declining, and with retired households underrepresented.

Figure 2a: Representation of age groups in the social rented sector

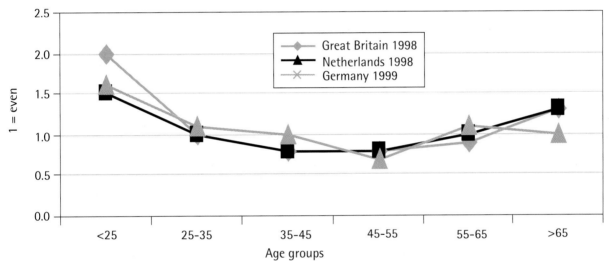

Source: Country experts; GB source = Family Spending

Figure 2b: Representation of age groups in the French social rented sector (1996)

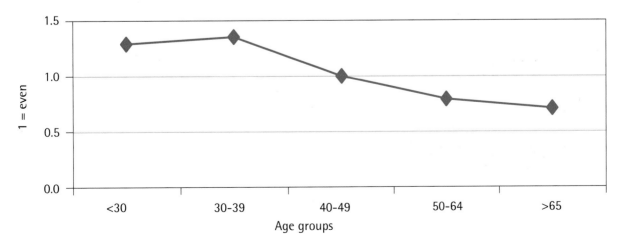

Source: Country expert

Figures 3a and 3b provide an analysis of the proportion of lone parents and nuclear families living in the social rented sector, compared to their representation in the population as a whole. It indicates that:

- In all the countries a greater proportion of lone parent households are housed in the social rented sector, but the proportion in Great Britain is the lowest compared to the population as a whole. It is highest in France where twice as many lone parents are housed in the social rented sector as are found in the population as a whole.
- Nuclear families are greatly underrepresented in the Dutch and Swedish social rented sectors. They are somewhat more numerous

in the British, French and German social rented sectors than in the population as a whole.

This examination of the representation of household types in the social rented sectors does not suggest that there is any distinguishing pattern in Britain that can explain the concentration of low income households in the British social rented sector. Nor does it appear that the 'equivalent' incomes of British households living in the social rented sector are systematically higher than the unadjusted figures suggest. In short, the British social rented sector houses more households from lower income groups than in France, Germany and the Netherlands.

Figure 3a: Representation of lone parent households in the social rented sector

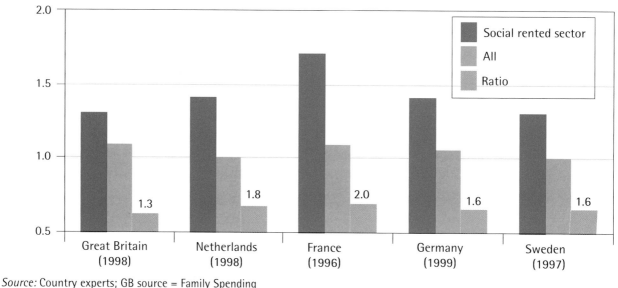

Source: Country experts; GB source = Family Spending

Figure 3b: Representation of nuclear families in the social rented sector

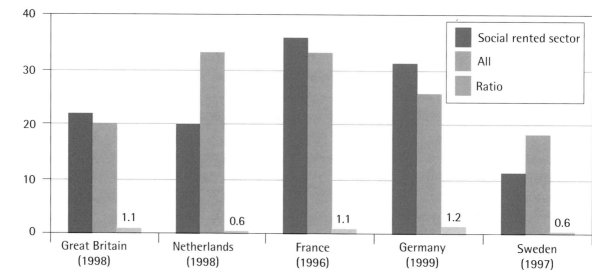

Source: Country experts; GB source = Family Spending

Income inequality

The analysis of the distribution of households from different income deciles throughout the tenures does not capture the full extent of potential residualisation in one important respect. It takes no account of income distribution generally. In other words, depending on the gap between households in the higher income deciles and the lower income deciles, the effect of inter-tenure polarisation may be smaller or greater than is implied by the initial analysis.

Figure 4a contains data on the extent of income inequality and poverty in the countries surveyed. Unfortunately, these data relate to 1994, and are the most recent that could be located. However, the most recent evidence suggests that inequality of disposable income rose in Britain in the late 1990s (Lakin, 2001, p 36). Figure 4 indicates that:

- Britain has the highest level of income inequality of the countries surveyed. This is caused principally by the very high proportion of households with very high incomes, and to a lesser extent by the number of households with low incomes.

- Inequality is lowest in the three Scandinavian countries. Again the principal cause of the lower level of inequality is the suppression of top-end incomes. Thus Denmark has almost the same proportion of households with low incomes as Britain.
- Germany, the Netherlands and France occupy an intermediate position in terms of inequality.
- Among the countries surveyed, Britain is the only one to have levels of inequality above the EU average. This reflects the greater levels of inequality in southern European countries omitted from this survey.

The impact of the tax and benefits systems in reducing poverty (here taken as an income below 50% of the average) is demonstrated in the second graph (in Figure 4b):

- Britain does not stand out as having an especially high level of pre-transfer poverty (although it is the highest among the countries surveyed and for which data is available, and slightly above the EU-12 average).
- However, Britain's tax and benefits system does notably less than in the other countries to raise the relative incomes of the poorest households, leaving a higher proportion of households in poverty than elsewhere.

Figure 4a: Poverty and riches: % households with disposable incomes 50% below or 200% above average incomes (1994)

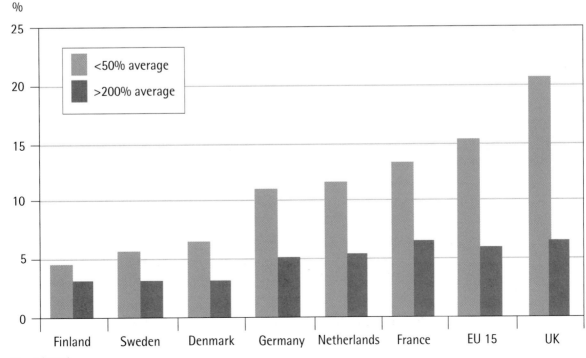

Source: Vogel (1997)

Figure 4b: Percentage of households in poverty before and after taxes and transfers (1993)

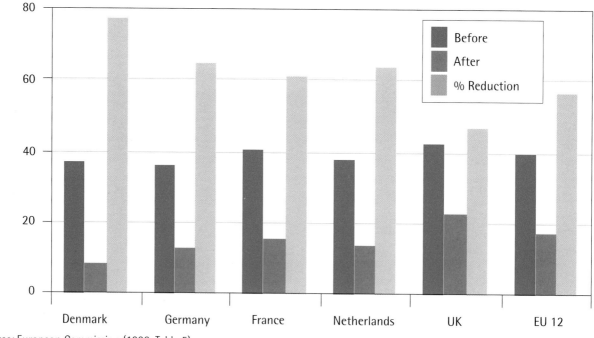

Legend:
- Before
- After
- % Reduction

Countries (left to right): Denmark, Germany, France, Netherlands, UK, EU 12

Source: European Commission (1998, Table 5)

Table 3, which uses more recent data, reveals that the high concentration of households from the lower income deciles in the British social rented sector combines with the higher levels of income inequality, to produce stark inter-tenure income divisions compared to the other countries:

- The incomes of Britain's social renters are substantially lower than the average.
- Even in Germany, where the social rented sector is concentrated in the former East Germany where incomes are lower than the average, social renters' incomes are much closer to the average than in Britain.
- Sweden is exceptional in that the incomes of private renters are identical to social renters. This may reflect the historic policy of promoting tenure neutrality and not recognising a 'social' rented sector as such.
- The incomes of owner occupiers are above the average in each of the countries.
- Britain's owner occupiers are not especially privileged, perhaps reflecting the high level of owner occupation.
- Swedish owner occupiers are, relatively speaking, the richest among the countries surveyed. This reflects the legal restrictions which limit owner occupation to houses in Sweden. The income of the group of households who have an equity stake in their flats through membership of an owner cooperative is 94% of the average.
- Strikingly the ratio of owner occupiers' incomes to social renters' incomes is very closely bunched at 1.5–1.7 in each of the countries except Britain where the ratio is 2.4.

Table 3: Incomes as percentage of average[a]

	Social renters	Owner occupiers	Private renters	All households	Owner occupiers: social renters (ratio)
France (1996)	76.2	116.8	82.4	100	1.5
Finland[b] (1997)	68.7	118.1	68.7	100	1.7
Germany (1999)	76.7	120.6	88.1	100	1.6
Great Britain (1997/98)	49.6	120.7	74.9	100	2.4
The Netherlands (1998)	72.2	123.0	84.1	100	1.7
Sweden (1997)	76.5	132.7	76.5	100	1.7

Notes: [a] After tax, except for France;
[b] The statistics for Finland do not distinguish between social and other renters. This is likely to exaggerate the incomes of social renters.
Source: country experts; GB = Family Spending

Exclusion and intra-tenure polarisation

The preceding analysis provides ample evidence of inter-tenure polarisation in terms of income in Britain. This seems to reflect the much greater importance attached to social rented housing as a safety net in Britain compared to other countries. It is likely that the need for such a safety net is linked to the much greater levels of income inequality in Britain. This is derived in part from the British labour market and also from the British social security system, which itself provides comparatively low levels of benefits with social insurance rates generally set below social assistance rates.

However, while the available data suggests that inter-tenure polarisation is less pronounced in the other countries studied, two other problems may be noted. The first is that a more socially mixed social rented sector may arise from the *exclusion* of vulnerable households from the sector. In some countries social landlords are reluctant to house the most deprived households, for financial and social reasons. In Denmark the tiny public rented sector, outside even the mainstream social sector, is used to house some of these households. In France, the private rented sector fulfils this role. These practices reflect the 'double bind' that social landlords face: the balance between good (financial) management and housing poor tenants, and the balance between helping the poorest households while avoiding residualisation (Blanc, 1998).

The second is that, although the countries studied experience less income polarisation between tenures, often qualitative evidence suggests that polarisation often occurs *within* the social rented sector.

In high-demand cities, such as Copenhagen and Stockholm, there is evidence of income polarisation within the social rented sector, with better off households living in older city-centre properties, and poorer tenants occupying newer flats in the suburbs. Stockholm's largest municipal housing company, Svenska Bostäder, which manages 50,000 dwellings, reports much higher concentrations of households with children in the outer suburbs. There is also a pronounced tendency for households from minority ethnic backgrounds to be concentrated in the outer suburbs. Half the households in the outer suburbs are from minority ethnic backgrounds, compared to one sixth in the inner city area (Svenska Bostäder, 2000). While residualisation in Britain is often attributed to widening income inequality, social scientists in Denmark are faced with explaining increased segregation within the social rented sector, despite decreases in income differentials over the past twenty years. The two strongest factors that help to identify concentrations of disadvantage in Denmark are welfare dependency and concentrations of the minority ethnic population (Skifter Andersen, 1999). However, these areas are far from being ghettos. Populations represent 'ethnic mosaics', in part arising from dispersal strategies adopted in the 1980s (Borresen, 1996). In Finland, however, intra-tenure polarisation appears to be limited either through strict income mixing on an estate basis, or by tenure mixing, sometimes within the same apartment block (ARA, 2000). This strategy implies a consistently high standard of housing, since better off households cannot be forced to live in a particular area or block.

Summary

The chapter has analysed the role that the social rented sector plays in the countries studied in some detail. The following conclusions can be drawn:

- The historic role of the social rented housing in meeting general housing shortages is largely over. However, its ability to meet shortages in high demand areas is often restricted generally by direct and indirect financial reasons.

- There is no evidence that housing systems are converging in terms of tenure patterns. There is no evidence of universal growth in the owner occupation sector or of decline in the social rented sector.

- The growth in owner occupation in Britain and the decline in the social rented sector in West Germany and Britain since 1980 reflect particular housing policies. In Germany's case social rented housing seems to have been designed to perform a temporary role of meeting shortages, while in Britain the purpose of the sector has been restricted to emphasise its function as a safety net.

- The examination of allocation systems suggested that while all systems attempt to meet affordability, need and safety net objectives to varying degrees, Britain places by far the most emphasis on the safety net function.

- Dutch 'choice'-based systems do not remove the dilemmas that arise from any allocation system. When they are accompanied by a change in 'currency' from need to the ability to wait, then they are likely to disadvantage vulnerable households.

- The role of Britain's social rented sector as a safety net is reflected in the much greater concentration of very low income households in the sector (adjusting for its size). Consequently, it has the character of a severely means-tested benefit, whereas its distribution is more evenly spread through income bands elsewhere, especially in France.

- Britain also has more income inequality than in the other countries, with the tax and benefits system doing less to mitigate earnings inequality. Consequently, the income differentials between social renters and owner occupiers in Britain are much greater than elsewhere.

- While the British system exhibits exceptionally high levels of inter-tenure polarisation, other forms of exclusion and polarisation exist elsewhere. For example, the lowest income groups are sometimes excluded from social rented housing in France, while the Danish and Swedish social rented sectors experience geographical polarisation within them as a result of allocation and pricing policies. The concentration of minority ethnic households in particular areas is often also a feature of such intra-tenure polarisation.

3

The provision of social rented housing

Introduction

Historically, social rented housing in Britain has been provided principally by local authorities, which both own and manage the housing. However, the municipal monopoly has gradually weakened over the past twelve years. After 1988 housing associations were promoted as the main providers of new social rented housing, while Large Scale Voluntary Transfers have diminished further the role of local authority housing. Nevertheless, three quarters of social rented housing in Britain remains under the direct ownership and management of local authorities.

The English Green Paper accepts the distinction established in the 1988 White Paper that the strategic role should be separated from the landlord. It proposes further transfers of up to 200,000 units a year, while seven Scottish local authorities, including Glasgow with a stock in excess of 90,000, are proposing to transfer their stocks. However, the English Green Paper proposes that the strategic and landlord functions can also be separated by the establishment of non-profit arms-length companies, whereby the local authority remains the legal owner of the housing stock, but does not have a majority on the board (DETR, 2000c).

This chapter describes the forms that social landlords take in the other countries covered in this survey.

Social landlords

The outstanding feature of the other countries studied in this survey is the near absence of social rented housing owned directly by local authorities. It plays a very minor role in Denmark, the Netherlands and Finland. In the case of the Netherlands, the remaining local authority housing is being transferred to housing associations. Nevertheless, there is no single model of social rented housing. Indeed, in the countries studied, four broad types of social landlord can be identified: municipal housing companies, housing associations, not-for-profit and for-profit companies (see Table 4).

Municipal housing companies

These are the main providers of social rented housing in Sweden (where they provide about 95% of social rented housing), Finland (63%) and Germany (more than 50%). They are given a higher level of operational autonomy than British local authority housing departments although the boards are appointed by the local authority. In Sweden the municipal housing companies take one of two forms: foundations with no shareholders; and companies in which the municipality owns the shares. The second model shares the proposed ownership structure for the formation of arms-length companies in England, although governance arrangements in Sweden allow the local authority to appoint the entire board. In all these countries there are often, though not always, more than one company in each local authority area. For example there are three in Stockholm. The size of some (such as SAGA in Hamburg with a stock of 100,000) are comparable with the largest local authorities in Britain. A degree of rationalisation is occurring in Finland, where a new company was often established for each new development. Partly for efficiency reasons, but also as part of the policy

Table 4: Types of social landlord

	Type of landlord	% of social rented sector owned by each landlord
Denmark	HA	>99
	LA	<1
Finland	MHC	63
	Organisation for social housing production	10
	Special needs housing organisation	8
	Industries, finance companies, insurance companies	7
	Other	12
France	HLM	
	OP/OPAC (LA controlled)	50
	SA (companies)	40
	Other	10
Germany	MHC	majority
	Other companies	
	Private landlords	
Netherlands	HA	99.3
	LA	0.7
Sweden	MHC	90-95
Great Britain	LA	77
	HA/RSL	23
England	LA	76.1
	RSL	23.9
Scotland	LA	83.4
	HA	16.6

Key: HA = housing association; LA = local authority; MHC = municipal housing company; HLM = *habitations à loyer modéré*; OP = *office public*; OPAC = *office public d'aménagement et de construction*; RSL = registered social landlord; SA = Société Anonyme

of introducing rent pooling, companies are merging into single ownership structures.

About 60% of French social rented housing is owned by organisations that are broadly speaking a weaker form of municipal housing company, in that local authorities do not have a majority of nominees on the board. In terms of governance, if not ownership, this arrangement comes closest to the arms-length companies proposed for England. These weaker forms of municipal housing companies in France come in two types. The majority (known as HLM-OPs) are formed by communes, municipalities or regions, and their boards are made up of representatives of local government (one third), central government (one third), tenants (one fifth) and representatives of

financial institutions (13%). There are also HLM-OPACs which tend to be larger than HLM-OPs. The boards of HLM-OPACs are larger than HLM-OPs (15 as opposed to seven), although the same interests are represented in roughly the same proportions.

Housing associations

Social landlords that operate in Denmark and the Netherlands are described as housing associations. They account for nearly all the social housing stock in these countries, although small public sectors still exist. There is no provision for profits to be distributed to shareholders within these organisations. The governance of the Dutch and Danish housing sectors is rather different. As in Britain, there is a trend among Dutch housing associations towards mergers, often within a group structure (see Chapter 6). An important feature of Danish housing associations is the financial autonomy of each estate, which is controlled by the tenants. (Local authorities have powers to intervene if tenants refuse to endorse prudent budgets.) Danish housing associations have often formed confederations in order to obtain central services efficiently, while maintaining their relatively small scale and autonomy.

Not-for- (or limited-) profit companies

These form an important component of the social rented sector in France, Finland and Germany. In France more than 40% of the social rented sector is provided by HLM-SAs, which are companies mainly sponsored by private sector firms or public enterprises. By law, tenant representation on the board is mandatory. Germany also has a tradition of employer and trade union-sponsored housing companies. In Finland some of the large national landlords were sponsored by various interest groups, such as the trade union federation (UUO), a large development company (SATO) and local government developers (YH Group). UUO and SATO have links to the Social Democratic and Conservative parties respectively. It should be noted that although such companies are described as 'not for profit', in fact those in Finland and Germany are permitted to make at least limited profits. Finnish housing companies are permitted to make a rate of return equivalent to two percentage points over the five year government bond rate. In Germany, before 1990, permitted rates of return depended on the level of investment. For a capital share of up to 15%, a rate of return of 4% was allowed. This rose to 6.5% for larger investments. Since 1990, these restrictions on the distribution of profits have been removed. In Finland, a new law has been introduced to prevent the housing companies from floating on the stock exchange (although shares can be sold privately).

For-profit private landlords

The most distinctive characteristic of the German system is the use of private landlords to provide social rented housing, with subsidies making up the difference between a 'social' and 'cost' rent (the cost rent allows for some rate of return). A dwelling passes into the 'pure' market rented sector once the subsidised loan has been repaid. This structure seems appropriate for a particular purpose, that is to promote building to remove a housing shortage. It seems inappropriate if the objective is to help to tackle enduring affordability or accessibility problems. The federal government withdrew subsidies from social rented housing in 1985, but reintroduced them in 1989 when housing shortages once again became acute. But the new subsidy scheme was designed to favour the private sector, and the shorter repayment period implied that the housing would pass from the social rented sector and into the market sector more rapidly than before. Now that many of the subsidised loans are being paid off, the social rented sector is shrinking quite quickly, and is now estimated to represent only 5% or 6% of the stock.

The so-called 'melting away' of a segment of the social rented sector can have major distributional effects. Initially, the market rent is often below the cost rent, but over time any surpluses accrued by the landlord are held within the private sector, with no public control over their use. This contrasts with the surpluses built up by Dutch, Danish and Swedish social landlords where surpluses may be used to benefit tenants (particularly in Denmark), to cross-subsidise new development (the Netherlands), or returned to the taxpayer (Sweden). Further, since municipal nomination rights are linked to subsidy, one can expect public authorities' ability to place vulnerable households in social rented housing to diminish over time.

Supervision and regulation

Social landlords are generally bound by rules relating to registration, regulation of activities, auditing, and supervision. In Britain there has traditionally been a divide between the housing association sector which has been quite closely regulated and supervised by the Housing Corporation in England and Scottish Homes, and the local authority sector which has been largely free of external scrutiny. This has changed in England with the establishment of the Housing Inspectorate. The Housing Inspectorate conducts 'best value' reviews concerning various aspects of local authorities' housing service, for example housing repairs and maintenance, strategy or homelessness service. Scottish Homes has been replaced by Communities Scotland – a single government agency which will act as a single regulator for the whole of the social rented sector.

In the 1990s there was a move to more liberal regimes in both Germany and the Netherlands. Following the bankruptcy of Germany's (indeed Western Europe's) largest social landlord (the trade union housing company, Neue Heimat; for an account see Power, 1993, ch 12), the federal government abolished the Law of the Public Good, so removing restrictions relating to the distribution of profits and the scope of activities that applied to housing companies. In the Netherlands, regulatory responsibility for housing associations was decentralised to local authorities under the Social Rented Management Order (BBSH) in 1993. The statute defines the scope of associations' operations, and their obligations to house defined target groups, consult tenants, maintain the quality of their stock and ensure financial continuity. This regime has suffered from the lack of formal sanctions on the part of local authorities and often a lack of resources with which to conduct effective scrutiny[1]. Consequently, a degree of re-centralisation is envisaged in the Housing Memorandum of 2000 (Remkes, 2000), with more precise guidance relating to the scope of housing association activities. This reflects the concerns of property companies which object to the diversification of housing association activity into commercial

[1] However, local authorities can refer housing associations to the Ministry of Housing whose ultimate sanction is the winding up of an association and the transfer of its properties to another association (Walker, 1998).

property development (often to cross-subsidise social housing). However, the government also suggests that associations should be obliged to diversify their social role to include the provision of supported accommodation, such as care homes for older people, an activity regarded as being risky by at least one credit rating agency.

In principle at least the French authorities exercise considerable scrutiny over the HLM-SAs, that is the social housing provided mainly by private and public employers. Financial scrutiny is carried out by the Caisse des Dépôts et Cosignations (the funding body for the HLMs) and the ministry. Their scope of activity is defined in their statutes, while an inter-ministerial public housing inspection task force, established in 1993, is empowered to check documentation and carry out on-site inspections. The French system of scrutiny therefore extends well beyond financial auditing and has led to a recent legal ruling that HLM-SAs qualify as public bodies for the purposes of public procurement (conclusions by Advocate General Jean Mischo, 19 October 2000: *Commission of the European Communities v The French Republic* [Case C-237/99]).

The growing importance of private finance has led to the emergence and rising importance of monitoring, which extends well beyond auditing, by finance bodies. The remit of the Housing Fund of Finland (ARA), formed in 1990, extends throughout the social rented sector, including municipal housing companies. It is responsible for supervising housing regulations to ensure competition, as well as designating and monitoring approved borrowers (ARA, 2000). Similarly, the Dutch Guarantee Fund (WSW) established in 1983 performs a quite extensive regulatory function. While WSW is concerned solely with the financial strength of housing associations, their operational activities influence the assessment of risk (see Chapter 5).

Finally, the social rented sector is increasingly coming under scrutiny from credit rating agencies, that perform quite extensive analyses of the financial strength of social landlords (both individually and as a sector) and the policy context within which they operate. Since these analyses help to determine the access and cost of funds, they might be expected to exert at least an indirect influence on social landlords and policy makers (see, for example, Standard & Poor's, 2000).

Summary

The main points that are relevant to the debate in Britain are:

- By moving away from local authority housing as a mode of provision, Britain is moving in a 'European' direction, although there is no homogenous 'European' form of provision.

- Municipal housing companies, housing associations, non-profit companies and private landlords are all used to provide social rented housing.

- The Netherlands, Sweden and Denmark have one dominant type of provider of social rented housing, while there are a variety of providers in Germany and Finland.

- Local monopolies are generally not a feature of social rented sectors in the countries surveyed. Even when there is one dominant type of provider, often more than one operates in each municipality.

- The use of private landlords to provide social rented housing seems appropriate to meet the objective of tackling housing shortages, but may be less appropriate for meeting long-term affordability or safety net objectives.

- The extent to which diversification is permitted varies according to the importance attached to risk avoidance.

- A variety of regulatory and supervisory mechanisms operate throughout Europe. Where private finance is used extensively, housing policy and social landlords have come under increasing scrutiny from external financial institutions, notably credit rating agencies.

Rent setting

4

Introduction

Rent setting at below market levels is a key feature of social rented housing. Some economists have always questioned the efficiency of setting rents below market levels arguing that the suppression of price signals is likely to distort the demand for social rented housing and may contribute to underoccupation and immobility. Such concerns partly motivated the long-term shift in the pattern of housing subsidy in Britain from supply-side to demand-side subsidies.

Nevertheless, after a long period of rises in the real level of rents, attention in Britain has begun to focus more on alleged pricing anomalies within the social rented sector:

- inconsistencies between regions;
- inconsistencies between social landlords, within the same region; and
- 'flat' rent structures within a landlord's stock, with rents failing to reflect fully differences in size, quality and location.

A divergence in rental policy is emerging between England and Scotland. The reform of rental structures is an important element of the reforms in England (DETR, 2000a, ch 9), but is so far absent from the Scottish agenda (Scottish Executive, 2000), although one may doubt how long the issue can be avoided given the link between rent restructuring and future Housing Benefit reform. Proposals for the reform of Housing Benefit, which is governed by a common set of regulations and is determined by the UK government, is intended to follow on from rent restructuring (in England). Housing Benefit is examined in the next chapter.

Supply-side subsidies and front-end loading

Rent setting in the social rented sector is generally driven by two factors that pull in opposite directions: the need to cover costs and the desire to provide affordable housing. Due to the heavily front-end loaded nature of housing costs, the gap between a cost-covering rent and an affordable rent is generally greatest when the dwelling is new. This is often met by subsidy, which can be withdrawn as rents rise, while loan repayments decline in real terms until eventually the loan is repaid. Periodically, new capital costs are likely to arise due to major repairs and renovation.

Subsidy systems are explored in more detail in Chapter 6, but a brief summary indicates the extent to which subsidy patterns conform to this pattern:

- In Denmark and Finland subsidy programmes based on diminishing interest rate subsidies are utilised.
- In Germany a subsidy which is withdrawn over time reduces 'cost rents' to 'social rents'.
- In France real interest rates are fixed, and are not stepped.
- Explicit subsidies have now been withdrawn in the Netherlands.
- In Sweden new subsidies have been reduced to the equivalent of a tax relief on interest payments.
- In Britain the principal subsidy mechanism for local authority housing has been recurrent revenue subsidies which have been reduced over time, and up-front capital grants for housing associations.

Rent setting at the level of the landlord

Anomalies within a landlord's stock can often arise from the differing age of the stock, with older stock enjoying lower levels of debt. In Britain local authorities and often housing associations have employed rent pooling to diminish anomalies between the rents on older and newer stock. Rent pooling really means pooling the debt associated with various housing developments over the whole of the landlord's stock.

Rent pooling is not used as extensively in the other countries covered in this study:

- In France and Germany the project-based nature of the finance system implies that rents are set on the basis of historic costs, although rent pooling has been permitted in Germany since 1988.
- Denmark operates a strict cost rental system, with rents set on the basis of historic costs at the level of the estate. The resultant anomalies, when combined with the allocation system that gives priority to the tenants of each estate (see Chapter 2), have adverse distributional implications, with better off tenants in Copenhagen reputedly paying lower rents in the more attractive city centre properties than the poorer tenants living in the less popular peripheral estates.
- Historic costs are the main driving force behind rents in Sweden, although rent pooling is permitted.
- In the Netherlands limited rent pooling is possible.
- The law governing Finnish social rented housing now states that the shareholder structure of housing companies must permit rent pooling. With an eye to using subsidies more efficiently the government favours 'rent equalisation', although the rate of progress varies between municipalities. Often rent equalisation necessitates the merger of municipal housing companies, especially when a separate company was established for each development.

The effectiveness of rent pooling in Britain has been enhanced by the existence of near monopoly social landlords operating in each local authority. The fragmentation of the British social rented sector, arising from the growth of housing associations, stock transfers, and the possible break up of local authority stocks on transfer creates the potential for anomalies to grow over time. In this sense the English attempts to set housing association and local authority rents within a common framework can be seen as an important bulwark against growing incoherence, although no formal mechanism for redistribution between landlords has been proposed. The government's strategy is now to reduce inconsistencies in rent structures by basing increases on a mix of local earnings (70%) and capital values (30%). Local authority rents will be permitted to rise relative to housing association rents with the objective of achieving coherence within a decade (DETR, 2000a).

Rent setting at the level of the property

The anomalies that arise from cost rental systems tend to mask further anomalies arising from rent structures. Nevertheless, the Dutch Rent Quality System, which sets a maximum differential for a series of property attributes, operates in much the same way as British 'points' schemes, and rent structures are reported to be relatively 'flat'. In Sweden, rents are determined by negotiations between tenants' associations and landlords. A Rent Tribunal exists to settle disputes having regard to the rents in properties with a similar 'use value' (which, like the British 'fair rent', assumes that the market is in balance). Nevertheless there are variations in the coherence of rent structures within Sweden. While Stockholm possesses some of the most anomalous rent structures, other cities, such as Gothenburg and Malmo, were reported to have more market-oriented rents policies. Indeed, in Gothenburg, rents in the suburban estates have been reduced, and increased in the inner city, in an attempt to let unpopular property.

Rent increases

Figure 5 illustrates the trends in rent levels in the social rented sectors in each of the countries surveyed, apart from Denmark.

Figure 5: Changes in real rents (1990-99)

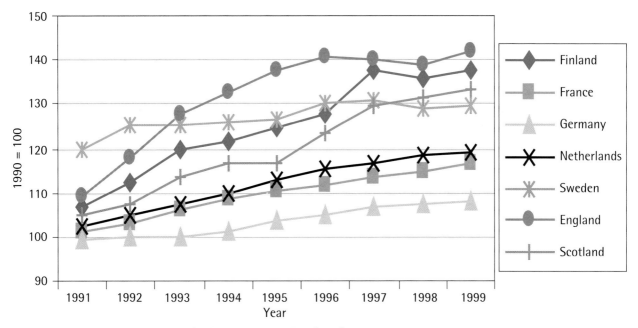

Source: Country experts; England and Scotland source = Wilcox (2000)

The figure shows that local authority tenants in England, Scotland, Finland and Sweden experienced noticeably larger real rent rises than tenants in the other countries. An exceptionally large rise in rents in 1991 accounts for most of the rise in Sweden. It is difficult to establish a clear link between the institutional arrangements that govern rent rises and the pattern indicated in the graph.

Rent increases in Sweden are determined by annual local negotiations between the tenants' associations and the municipal housing companies. In effect, cost rental principles apply in Germany, Finland and Denmark, subject to provisions for modest profits to be made in Finland and Germany. Government influence over rent rises is indirect, for example arising from the way in which interest subsidies are formulated. The French housing ministry issues guidance, although landlords retain freedom over rent setting.

Central government plays a significant role in establishing rent rises in the Netherlands and Britain. The Dutch government lays down annual increases for the sector, although housing associations are able to vary the increase between dwellings, subject to an upper limit. British governments have issued guidance to local authorities, which encourages a certain minimum increase should the local authority wish to avoid financial penalty (since subsidy levels are determined with reference to guideline rents). However, deviation from guideline rents does occur. Housing association rents on pre-1988 tenancies fall within the 'fair rent' regime of rents set administratively by rent officers. However, rent officers normally accept housing association guidance. Housing associations are in principle free to set rents on post-1988 rents, in accordance with their costs. In Scotland, Scottish Homes (now Communities Scotland) expected associations to follow three broad and potentially conflicting principles: affordability, comparability with other social landlords and cost-covering. However, The Housing Corporation has attempted to 'influence' the rents of English associations since 1996, and has more recently recommended real rises no higher than 1%. Although legally associations retain autonomy over rent setting, they might be influenced by the fear of losing future development funding should they break the Corporation's guidance. The English Green Paper suggested that inflation-only increases should become the norm for housing associations, although this has now been altered to a proposed 0.5% real increase (DETR 2000a, 2000c, 2001b).

Such direct political control over rent setting can be problematic in an increasingly market-oriented environment. This is particularly the case with stock transfer associations in England. The capricious nature of government rent setting policy is illustrated by the Netherlands, where one set of assumptions on rent increases was used to calculate payments to associations under the 'grossing and balancing' exercise (see page 43), yet within a few years much lower rent increases have been imposed on the sector. Indeed inflation only increases are now the policy of the Dutch government. Such rent restrictions have been highlighted by the credit rating agency Moody's as a factor that might lead to neglect of long-term maintenance (Moody's Investment Services, 1999).

Summary

This survey has shown that:

- Rent structures in other countries share many of the anomalies found in Britain.

- The fragmentation of the social rented sector in some countries can lead to still greater anomalies.

- As the British social rented sector becomes more diverse, the case for a common legal and rent setting framework is strengthened.

5

Housing allowances

Introduction

One of the main reasons why British governments have sought to limit rent rises in recent years has been to curb the cost of Housing Benefit. Having succeeded in limiting the cost of Housing Benefit, the emphasis in reform proposals has shifted towards a desire to improve its structure. Its principal structural deficiencies fall into three areas:

1. Housing Benefit contributes to the poverty trap. This is caused by its high 'taper', or rate of withdrawal, as income rises.
2. About 60% of tenants in receipt of Housing Benefit make no contribution to their housing costs (Kemp, 2000, p 52). Housing Benefit pays all the eligible rent of tenants whose incomes are at or below the social assistance level[1]. Some commentators argue that tenants should make at least some contribution to their housing costs.
3. Housing Benefit completely insulates recipients from changes in housing costs, so obliterating any price signals that might encourage a more efficient use of the stock. This is caused by the formula which is designed to protect tenants' post-rent incomes, so if rents rise by £1, benefit rises by £1.

The government has indicated that the reform of Housing Benefit should await the reform of rent structures (in England). The objective appears to be that together rent and Housing Benefit reform

should create a social market in social housing, whereby price signals assume a greater role within the context of generally sub-market rents. This chapter assesses the scope for reform by examining the British system in a European context. It should be noted that data and discussions of reform proposals relate to the social rented sector. Rather different conditions apply in the private rented sector.

Housing allowance systems

Each of the countries surveyed has established systems of housing allowances, but their coverage and structure vary:

Coverage

In four of the countries (Finland, France, Germany and Sweden) both owner occupiers and tenants are entitled to claim housing allowance. However, some provision is made for owner occupiers in other countries. In Denmark, loans are available for owners, in the Netherlands a parallel system of support operates for owner occupiers (OECD, 1998a), and in Britain social assistance payments are enhanced to support mortgage interest payments, after a waiting period (Kemp, 1997, 2000).

Separate schemes for pensioners operate in Denmark, Finland, and Sweden. Finland also operates a separate system for students (OECD, 1998b). The French scheme for pensioners (ALS) also covers long-term unemployed people, and people with disabilities. Separate schemes operate for families with children (ALF) and for households living in accommodation supported

---

[1] In the social rented sector, households with non-dependants do not have all their rent covered by Housing Benefit. In the private rented sector some two thirds of claimants do not receive benefit based on their full rent because it is judged to be too high.

by subsidised loans (APL). Allowances are nevertheless calculated on a unified principle.

Generally all adults are entitled to claim housing allowances, but in Sweden childless claimants aged 29–65 were excluded from eligibility in 1996 to cut back on rising costs, and in Britain most full-time students have been ineligible since 1990 (Kemp, 2000).

Safety net and affordability objectives

Housing allowance systems are structured with essentially two objectives:

1. To improve the affordability of housing.
2. To provide a safety net that prevents post-housing cost incomes falling below a certain level[2].

The relative importance attached to each of these objectives varies between countries. Often the housing allowance system is used to secure the first objective, while the social assistance system is relied on to meet the second objective. Table 5 indicates the main structural features of housing allowance systems and their interaction with social assistance. Three approaches can be identified:

1. The British social assistance system does not make any allowance for rents. In order to prevent post-rent incomes falling below the social assistance level, recipients of social assistance benefits have all their rent met by Housing Benefit. As net incomes rise, benefit is withdrawn at a rate of 65%, a much steeper taper than in other countries, implying that assistance does not rise very far up the income scale. Consequently, the British housing allowance system is primarily devoted to

meeting the safety net objective, rather than the affordability objective[3].

2. Sweden, Finland and Denmark provide examples of countries where the housing allowance system has affordability objectives, whereas the social assistance system acts as a safety net to protect post-rent incomes. The taper is no higher than 33%. Eligibility for housing allowances must be tested *before* social assistance is claimed. Consequently, childless claimants in Sweden who lost eligibility to housing allowance in 1996 received protection from the social assistance system.

3. In the Netherlands housing allowances mainly perform an affordability function, while social assistance is intended to provide a safety net. However, since social assistance provides only standard allowances for housing costs, it appears possible that post-rent incomes could fall below the social assistance level.

4. Germany's system is a hybrid of the Dutch and Scandinavian systems. Two systems of housing allowance (*Wohngeld*) operate in Germany. *Tabellenwohngeld* aims to assist tenants with affordability by limiting housing costs to 20% of income. The affordability objective is indicated by the relatively low rate of withdrawal (21%). *Pauschaliertes Wohngeld* is paid automatically as a lump sum to social assistance recipients. The latter performs a hybrid role of part affordability and part safety net. However, if rents threaten post-rent income, a further safety net payment from social assistance is possible.

Because the British system of housing allowance performs primarily a safety net function, it is clear why it contains the structural deficiencies outlined above:

- The majority of tenants make no contribution to housing costs because their social security benefits make no allowance for rent. Housing Benefit has to pay all the rent to protect post-rent incomes falling below the poverty line.
- The complete insulation of Housing Benefit recipients in the social rented sector from changes in rent also arises from the objective of protecting post-rent incomes.

---

[2] Kemp (2000) provides a slightly different typology; see especially p 48.

[3] The reform of British Housing Benefit in 1988 can be seen as a narrowing of its objective from performing both affordability and safety net functions to one which is primarily about providing a safety net. Thus the pre-1988 system distinguished between recipients of social assistance (so-called 'certificated' claimants) and other claimants (for whom another formula was used). The post-1988 system restricted eligibility further up the income scale and so became predominantly a safety net.

Table 5: Housing allowances (HA) and social assistance (SA)

	Maximum rent paid under HA or SA (%)	Taper (% net income)	Treatment of housing costs in social assistance
Denmark	75	16-27	Rent in excess of HA added to SA
Finland	<80	28	Rent in excess of HA & some other housing costs are added to SA
France	80	-	-
Germany	100	21	Rent in excess of HA is added to payment rates & is conditional on receipt of at least part of SA
NL	80	progressive 0-100	Housing costs exceeding individual subsidies are supposed to be covered by standard SA rates
Sweden	30-75	10-33 (depending on family type)	Rent in excess of HA is added to SA payment rates
UK	100	65 (for people not receiving SA)	100% of rent is covered by HA for SA claimants

Source: OECD 1998c, Table 2.5

- The poverty trap is so severe because it pays the whole rent of the very poorest households and is then withdrawn quickly because it is intended to protect the very poorest households, rather than promote affordability of rather better off households.

Trends in dependence on housing allowances

Figure 6 provides a standardised index to indicate changes in the numbers of people claiming housing allowances since 1990. It should be remembered that these data relate to all claimants, including private tenants and owner occupiers where they are entitled to make a claim. Figure 6 shows that:

- There has been no general inexorable rise in the *numbers* of recipients of housing allowance since 1990.
- France and West Germany exhibit steady increases in the numbers depending on housing allowances in the 1990s. There may have been some reductions in the numbers since the most recent data (1997 for France; 1998 for West Germany) as unemployment has fallen.

Figure 6: Changes in numbers claiming housing allowances

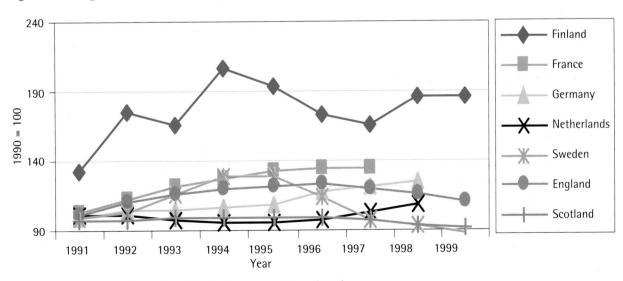

Source: Country experts; England and Scotland source = Wilcox (2000)

- Claimant numbers in Sweden and England rose substantially in the first half of the 1990s and then declined, in part reflecting falling unemployment. In the case of Sweden, restrictions on eligibility for housing allowance (as discussed earlier) and the introduction of a more severe taper also contributed to falling claimant numbers.
- In the Netherlands, claimant numbers fell in the early to mid-1990s, and then rose modestly, while they remained steady in Scotland, before falling in the latter part of the decade.
- Claimant numbers in Finland soared in the first half of the 1990s, reflecting that country's severe economic crisis. Although numbers peaked in 1994, the increase in numbers receiving housing allowances remains greater than in any of the other countries surveyed.

Despite these diverse patterns in the numbers claiming benefit, Figure 7 indicates a more consistent pattern in housing allowance expenditure trends:

- In all five of the countries for which data was available the real costs of housing allowances were higher at the end of the period than at the start.
- Sweden is the only country to have achieved significant reductions in the cost of housing allowances. Having risen by more than 40% in

real terms from 1990–94, they had almost returned to their 1990 level by 1999. These reductions are attributable to the cuts in benefit entitlement outlined above and falling unemployment.
- France and the Netherlands experienced large increases in real expenditure on housing allowances – around 60% and 40% respectively.
- Britain registered the second largest increase in expenditure on housing allowances, after Finland. The 90% real increase in expenditure in Britain is surprising given that increases in claimant numbers were relatively modest. However, it is notable that England and Finland experienced the biggest rises in social rents in the 1990s, and these would undoubtedly contribute to rising dependency on housing allowances (see Chapter 4, Figure 5).

Levels of dependence on housing allowances

The analysis so far has highlighted *trends* in the numbers of recipients of housing allowances and their cost. Figure 8 indicates the *proportion* of tenants in the social rented sector who receive housing allowances:

Figure 7: Real cost of housing allowances (1990-99)

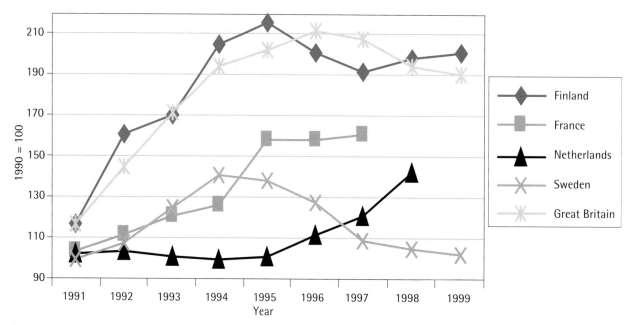

Source: Country experts; England and Scotland source = Wilcox (2000)

Figure 8: Proportion of social rented tenants receiving housing allowances

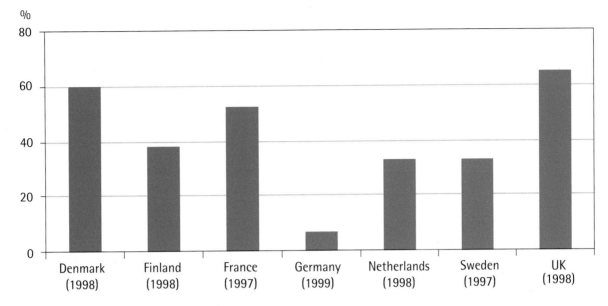

Source: Country experts; UK source = author's estimates

- Almost two thirds of social tenants in Britain receive housing allowances. This is the highest proportion in any of the countries surveyed, and is substantially higher than in all the other countries, other than Denmark.
- The high proportion of social tenants in receipt of housing allowances in Denmark is attributable to the generous scheme operated for pensioners.
- Only one third of social tenants in the Netherlands and Sweden are in receipt of housing allowances.
- Just under 40% of social tenants in Finland and just over one half in France receive housing allowances.

Figure 9 indicates that the level of expenditure on housing allowances (expressed as a share of GDP) is also the highest in Britain:

- Britain devotes 1.8% of GDP to housing allowances.
- Sweden is the only other country to devote more than 1% of GDP to housing allowances, but Britain's expenditure is still 1.5 times the Swedish equivalent.
- Britain spends twice as much on housing allowances as Denmark and France; four times as much as Finland; more than five times as much as the Netherlands; and more than 10 times as much as Germany.

Figure 9: Housing allowance expenditure as % of GDP (1995)

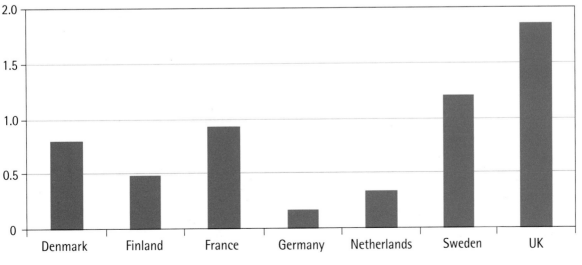

Source: International Social Security Reform Monitor

Some of the difference between Britain's levels of housing allowance dependency and expenditure may be explained by the different relationship between housing allowances and social assistance. Where social assistance is enhanced to meet high housing costs, this will not be measured as housing allowance expenditure (but note that this is what happens with Income Support for Mortgage Interest (ISMI) in Britain).

However, the most obvious causes of high housing benefit dependence relate to social and economic factors:

- the greater concentration of low income households in the British social rented sector (see Chapter 2, Figure 1a);
- the greater pre- and post-tax and benefit inequality in Britain (see Chapter 2, Figure 4b);
- the social security system (see below).

Thus Housing Benefit reform in Britain cannot be considered in isolation from:

- *Labour market inequalities:* Despite comparatively low levels of unemployment, work is distributed very unevenly in Britain. Work has polarised between households with no one in work and households with all adult members in work (see Table 6). Britain has an exceptionally high proportion of workless households with children. Moreover, the

authors of a recent study of worklessness commented that "Perhaps the most striking incidence of inactivity is among men resident in social housing; of these, 20% are inactive and only 54% are in work" (Dickens et al, 2001, p 14).

Table 6: Employment polarisation

	Year	Germany	France	Netherlands	UK
Workless	1983	15.0[a]	12.5	20.6[b]	16.0
	1990	12.8	14.4	17.2	14.3
	1994	15.5	16.5	17.2	18.9
Mixed	1983	32.5	30.6	39.1	30.1
	1990	27.7	28.3	31.9	22.0
	1994	25.6	27.9	27.0	18.6
All work	1983	52.5	56.9	40.3	53.9
	1990	59.5	57.4	50.9	63.7
	1994	58.9	55.7	55.7	62.1

Notes: [a] = 1984; [b] = 1985
Source: Gregg and Wadsworth (1996, Table 1)

- *Social security systems:* Britain's social security system is markedly less generous than those operated in the other countries surveyed, even when relative per capita income is taken into consideration (Table 7). Britain's social insurance system largely pays benefits below social assistance rates, whereas social insurance benefits are typically earnings-related in the other countries. Consequently, Britain has a greater dependence on social

Table 7: Levels of benefit for unemployed claimants (1995)

	Unemployment insurance		Social assistance			
	Single household	Single household	Single household	Couple + 2 children	Lone parent + 2 children	
	Payment rate (%)	Maximum amount[a] (UK = 100)	Maximum amount[a] (UK = 100)	Maximum amount[a] (UK = 100)	Maximum amount[a] (UK = 100)	GDP per capita[b] (UK = 100)
Denmark	90	427	256	138	169	121
Finland	80	–	112	137	129	100
France	75	1499	116	99	104	112
Germany	60	754	95	116	118	115
Netherlands	70	697	213	123	136	111
Sweden	80	408	115	130	120	105
UK	Flat rate	100	100	100	100	100

Notes:
[a] Calculated from US$ equivalent; currency conversions based on purchasing power parities
[b] 1995, using purchasing power parities
Sources: *derived from OECD (1998c), Tables 2.3 and 2.9; Eurostat*

assistance benefits, and even these are generally less generous than their equivalents in the other countries. The British state pension is similarly lacking in generosity, and is a cause of a high level of pensioner dependence on means-tested benefits. Since means-tested social assistance benefits are paid at low levels, the housing allowance system plays a much greater role in Britain, as is illustrated in Table 8. Data from 1992 suggest that, after housing costs, incomes of British social assistance recipients (in relation to average earnings) were similar to France and Germany, but much lower than their counterparts in the countries surveyed in this report (Wilcox, 1998, Table 3.)

Table 8: Composition of incomes of unemployed benefit recipients

Single person

Country & month of benefit receipt	UI	UA	SA	FB	HA	IT	Total
DK 1	156	0	0	0	0	-56	100
DK 60	0	0	83	0	38	-21	100
Fin 1	124	–	0	0	7	-31	100
Fin 60	0	60	17	0	33	-10	100
F 1	105	0	0	0	4	-9	100
F 60	0	72	0	0	32	-4	100
D 1	99	0	0	0	1	0	100
D 60	0	99	0	0	1	0	100
NL 1	158	0	0	0	0	-58	100
NL 60	0	0	109	0	21	-30	100
Sw 1	152	0	0	0	0	-52	100
Sw 60	0	0	93	0	7	0	100
UK 1	44	0	0	0	56	0	100
UK 60	0	0	44	0	56	0	100

One earner couple with two children

Country & month of benefit receipt	UI	UA	SA	FB	HA	IT	Total
DK 1	98	0	0	13	15	-26	100
DK 60	0	0	135	10	0	-45	100
Fin 1	88	0	0	22	14	-24	100
Fin 60	0	40	33	14	20	-7	100
F 1	76	0	0	9	19	-4	100
F 60	0	46	4	14	38	-2	100
D 1	83	0	0	7	10	0	100
D 60	0	71	9	7	13	0	100
NL 1	124	0	0	9	6	-39	100
NL 60	0	0	98	10	14	-22	100
Sw 1	112	0	0	15	12	-39	100
Sw 60	0	0	74	12	0	0	100
UK 1	50	0	0	12	38	0	100
UK 60	0	0	55	11	34	0	100

Key: UI = unemployment insurance; UA = unemployment assistance; SA = social assistance; FB = family benefits; HA = housing allowance; IT = income tax
Source: OECD (1998c) Tables 3.2-3.5

Benefit reforms introduced by the Labour government have improved the financial position of some households in low paid work (through Working Families Tax Credit) and among poor pensioners (through the Minimum Income Guarantee that effectively uprates pensioner Income Support more quickly than prices). However, so long as rents rise in real terms and other benefits (such as Job Seekers' Allowance) rise only in line with inflation, the dependence of households in receipt of Housing Benefit will continue to grow. If lower-end earnings lag behind rent increases, then the numbers receiving Housing Benefit are likely to rise.

Thus the introduction of so-called 'shopping' incentives by making tenants pay a minimum contribution to their rent would have to be carefully designed to prevent the possibility of post-rent incomes falling below social assistance levels (see Kemp's (1998) proposals for a Housing Benefit based on 90% of eligible rent relate to the private rented sector in the first instance). The higher the 'benchmark rent', which would form the basis of enhancements to social assistance benefits, the lower the numbers who would face this predicament, although it would still be a possibility[3].

With the benchmark there is a clear trade-off between the cost of the scheme and the probability of a tenant's post-rent income falling below social assistance levels. While the extent to which small shopping incentives would affect tenants' behaviour is uncertain, there may be some distributional benefit if subsidies associated with social rented housing were allocated regressively. This could arise if unfair allocation systems systematically place the poorest households in the least popular accommodation,

and 'flat' rent structures lead the poorest tenants to subsidise the rather better off tenants[4].

Other choices include the introduction of the 'dual taper' system that meets all the rent for very low income tenants, but better off tenants are expected to make some contribution, although the taper is more gradual, so weakening the poverty trap (see, for example, Hills, 1991, ch 10). Such a reform would indicate a broadening of the scope of Housing Benefit to meet both safety net and affordability objectives.

Summary

This chapter has reviewed the role played by housing allowances in six European countries. It indicates that there is relatively little scope for the reform of Housing Benefit without increasing costs for the following reasons:

- The apparent deficiencies in the British Housing Benefit system arise from its evolution into playing the role of safety net, that is, to prevent post-rent incomes falling below social assistance levels.

- This role arises because British tenants have a high dependence on social assistance, in part because worklessness is unevenly distributed but also because the rates of social insurance benefit and the state pension in Britain are set below social assistance levels. Moreover, social assistance is set at levels that do not contain any allowance for housing costs.

---

[3] An option presented in the DETR's Green Paper suggests that benchmark could be based on 'average housing costs for the area and household size' (2000b, para 11.70). This would be likely to create a large number of losers; see Kemp's proposal that it 'should be set at an amount below which it is possible for all housing benefits to find accommodation in their locality' (1998, p 3).

[4] Kemp (1998) suggests that rent structures would have to be reformed before his scheme could be extended to the social rented sector. Unpublished calculations by Findlay, Stephens and Houston found evidence of flat rent structures in Scotland, but that economic subsidies to tenants (defined as the difference between market rents and actual gross rents) are distributed progressively in the housing association sector and evenly in the local authority sector.

6

Financing social rented housing: subsidies and surpluses

Introduction

As described in Chapter 2, social rented housing has been promoted for a variety of reasons, including the removal of housing shortages and the promotion of affordability. Each of these objectives is achieved by lowering the cost of provision through subsidy systems.

Supply-side subsidies commonly attempt to lower the burden of housing debt, especially in its early years when it is greatest. The real cost of loan repayments is generally highest in the early years of the loan because (in western Europe at least) loans are fixed in nominal terms, so both the real value of the loan and its repayments diminish in real terms over time. This 'front-end loading' problem tends to be exacerbated when inflation is high, because both nominal and real interest rates tend to rise with inflation. However, high inflation also diminishes the real value of debt and debt repayments more quickly.

We have seen (in Chapter 2) that social rented sectors are maturing, in the sense that the era of large scale building programmes designed to meet general housing shortages is over. As a social sector matures it is likely to tend towards surplus, even if subsidies have been withdrawn because the rate of loan repayment exceeds the rate of loan acquisition[1].

The chapter begins with a brief overview of the changing macroeconomic environment affecting housing finance. It then goes on to examine the structure of supply-side subsidies for social rented housing, and the provisions for redistributing rent surpluses.

The macroeconomic environment

Over the past two decades, monetary indicators in the industrialised economies have tended to converge. This means that, although so-called *real* indicators (those that measure things such as economic growth and unemployment) continue to vary greatly between countries, inflation and interest rates have tended to fall and converge. Explanations for this phenomenon include:

- greater stability in the world economy, notably the diminished importance of oil price shocks;
- informal pressures operating through globalised financial markets that lead governments to pursue policies that promote low inflation often turning to active monetary policies (for a discussion of globalisation and housing in the industrialised economies, see United Nations Centre for Human Settlements [HABITAT], 2001, ch 8); and

---

[1] There are exceptions. These tend to arise when at least some of the following factors combine: large and relatively recent building programmes leading to high levels of outstanding debt; low quality building requiring extensive maintenance or demolition; long-term poor maintenance leading to the need for renovation or demolition; and low demand caused by the poor quality of the stock, social changes or depopulation, often leading to demolition. In such circumstances a relatively high historic debt may become concentrated on fewer and fewer tenants.

Figure 10: Trends in inflation (1980-2000)

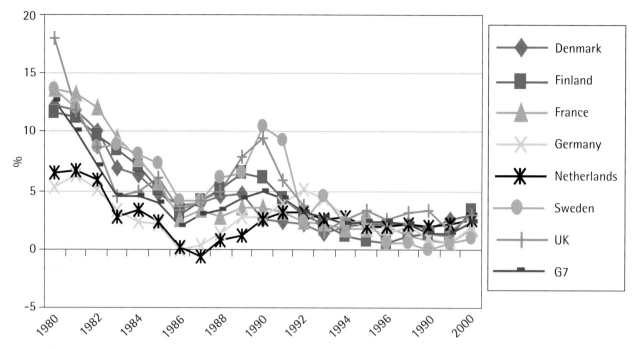

Source: HM Treasury

- formal pressures within the European Union, such as the Maastricht 'convergence criteria' for membership of the single currency and the Growth and Stability Pact, that require member governments to pursue low inflation policies and to limit fiscal deficits[2].

Figure 10 indicates the strength of the trend towards lower inflation, not only in the European Union, but throughout the industrialised world (represented by the Group of 7 [G7] of industrialised countries). The impact of the oil price shock in the early 1980s is clear and the strong downward trend in inflation in the 1990s striking. Moreover, the variation in inflation rates has been reduced considerably. (The standard deviation in inflation rates in the countries surveyed plus the G7 as a whole fell from 3.1 in 1990 to 0.8 in 2000.)

Figure 11 indicates a similar downward trend in nominal interest rates. It is notable that since

long-term interest rates reflect expectations of future inflation, the financial markets clearly expect low inflation to be sustained.

Trends in fiscal policy require more careful interpretation. The Maastricht Treaty implied the need for fiscal restraint in the European Union. Figure 12 appears to indicate such a fiscal tightening since around 1993-94, to the extent that several countries, including Britain, have moved into budgetary surplus. Furthermore, there have been examples of reductions in housing subsidies in the 1990s. Cuts in interest subsidies in Sweden, the ending of construction subsidies in the Netherlands, and the phasing out of mortgage interest relief in Britain, each provide examples of fiscal consolidation related to the housing sector. But such trends are not universal, and the European Central Bank (ECB) and its predecessor, the European Monetary Institute (EMI), have repeatedly complained that European governments have not improved their underlying budgetary positions. Reductions in deficits have largely depended on cyclical factors, notably reduced debt service charges as interest rates have fallen[3].

---

[2] The convergence criteria related to inflation, long-term interest rates, exchange rate stability, and the avoidance of excessive deficits (see Stephens, 1998). The Stability and Growth Pact formalises the provisions of the Maastricht Treaty relating to excessive deficits. All member states are obliged to avoid such deficits [normally defined as 3% of GDP for current deficits], but material sanctions are restricted to members of the single currency (see Stephens, 1999). Of the countries included in this survey, Germany, France, Finland and the Netherlands have joined the euro.

[3] For example: "Active consolidation measures do not appear to have played an active role in improving the underlying budgetary positions in 1999" (ECB, 2000, p 37; see also EMI, 1998).

Figure 11: Long-term interest rates

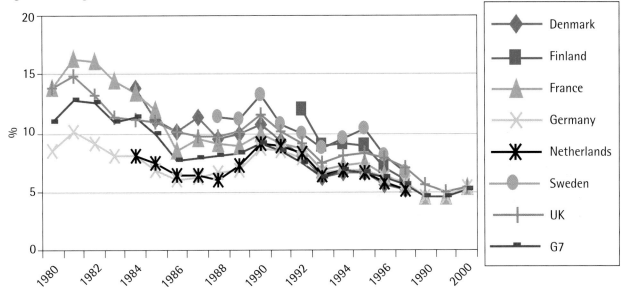

Source: HM Treasury

Figure 12: Government fiscal balances (1990-99) (+ = surplus/ − = deficit)

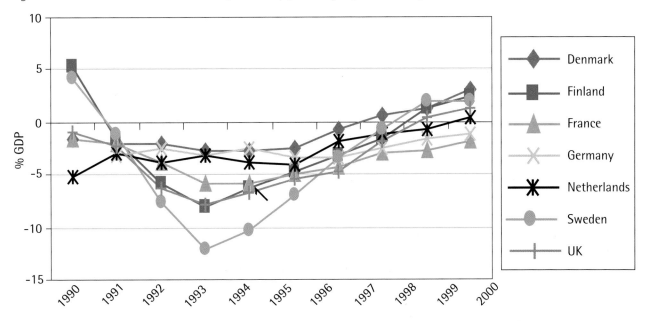

Source: European Monetary Institute/European Central Bank

This implies future budgetary consolidation if the principles on which the single currency was founded are to be upheld.

Subsidy systems

In this section the various subsidy instruments are outlined.

State loans

State loans were once a familiar policy instrument, being widely used in the Netherlands, Sweden, to some extent in Germany, as well as in Britain. Public expenditure concerns have led to their removal in Britain, the Netherlands and Sweden, and they now have a much-diminished role in Germany. Nevertheless, they remain the principal source of finance in Finland and France.

The Housing Fund of Finland

The Housing Fund of Finland (ARA) was established in 1990 as a government agency. It is arms-length from the government, but is not independent. Its Board is appointed by the Council of State. ARA has a series of funding and regulatory functions.

Regulatory functions include:

- registering designated borrowers

- monitoring designated borrowers (credit and liquidity checks)

- controlling the price and quality of state-subsidised construction

Financial functions include:

- granting ARAVA (state) loans and approving interest subsidies

- allocating repair and other housing grants

While the fund is not independent its balance sheet is separate from the state budget. The fund is financed almost entirely through loan repayments and the securitisation of state loans. There have been no grants from government for at least the last six years.

Housing Fund of Finland: sources of income

%	1995	1996	1997	1998	1999	2000 (est.)
Loan repayment	74.1	76.8	97.9	71.6	68.1	55.6
Budget transfer	0	0	0	0	0	0
Securiti-sation	25.9	21.7	0.0	26.9	31.4	44.2
Other	0	1.5	2.1	1.5	0.5	0.3
Total	100	100	100	100	100	100

Source: ARA

In Finland, state loans (still known as ARAVA, an acronym for the long-since abolished committee established to provide them) fund more than half the units of subsidised housing. The nominal interest rate on ARAVA loans is currently set at 3.8%, and increased annually by 1% of the interest rate plus inflation until a ceiling has been reached[4].

They have been financed by bond issues made by a government agency, the Housing Fund of Finland (ARA), but more recently the securitisation of ARAVA loans has provided sufficient revenue to finance new loans (see Chapter 7). The operation of the Housing Fund is outlined in the box above.

The French system of state loans is still characterised by a special finance circuit with the state-owned Caisse des Dépots et Cosignations (CDC) acting as a conduit for privileged funds from tax-exempt savings accounts (*Livret A*) run exclusively by the savings banks. Interest rates are fixed at 3.55% on mainstream PLA-funded housing and 3.45% on PLUS-funded housing for low income households.

Capital grants

Capital grants which reduce the cost of development that requires loan finance are the central subsidy for housing associations/registered social landlords in Britain where, on average, they still meet more than half the construction costs.

[4] If inflation is 2%, the interest rate for the second year of the loan is set as follows: (0.03 3.8) + 3.8 = 3.194%. The interest rate is increased until it reaches 3.7% in *real* terms. With 2% inflation, this occurs in around year 14. Until then the real interest rate is less than 3.7% and varies according to inflation. Consequently, the subsidy is concentrated in the early years of the loan.

A much smaller level of grant is provided in Denmark by the municipalities. Until recently this was set at 7% of costs, but central government has raised it to 14% to provide an incentive for municipalities to control the size of development programmes, now that central government no longer sets quotas.

Central, regional and local government in France contribute varying amounts to the capital costs of projects. Under the PLA scheme a government grant of 12.7% was available (1991–96), but this has been superseded by a reduction in VAT from 19.6% to 5.5%. Grants are also employed in Germany, but only in the *Länder* of the former East. They are not used in the other countries included in this survey.

Revenue subsidies

As with British local authority housing, recurrent revenue subsidies have been the main subsidy mechanism in the German system. However, in Germany the subsidy is more precisely formulated. Since the 1950s the level of subsidy has been determined by the difference between a 'cost rent' (which allows for construction costs,

management and maintenance, arrears and voids and a 4% rate of return) and a 'social rent' which is set according to the incomes of the target group. Over a 15 year period the subsidy is reduced as the social rent rises towards, and eventually meets, the cost rent. A similar outcome can be achieved through state loans, but the system is now mainly reliant on free market loans. Recurrent subsidies have also played a secondary role in the Netherlands until their recent abolition.

Interest subsidies

Interest subsidies are the central subsidy instrument in Denmark and Sweden, while an interest subsidy programme was introduced in Finland in the 1990s, in parallel to the ARAVA state loan system.

In Denmark, the government bears the interest rate risk, since payments are fixed according to a formula, whereby rents cover 3.6% of costs in the first year, rising by 75% of the annual inflation rate. Over time, if the interest rate rises above the market rate, the government may begin to recoup its earlier investment.

Diagram 1: The existing system of redistributing surpluses in Denmark

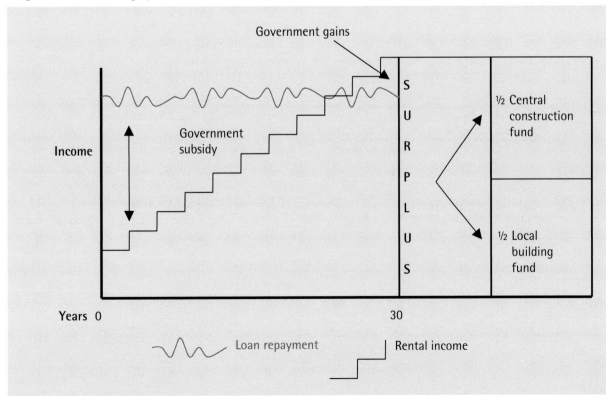

Diagram 2: The new system of redistributing surpluses in Denmark

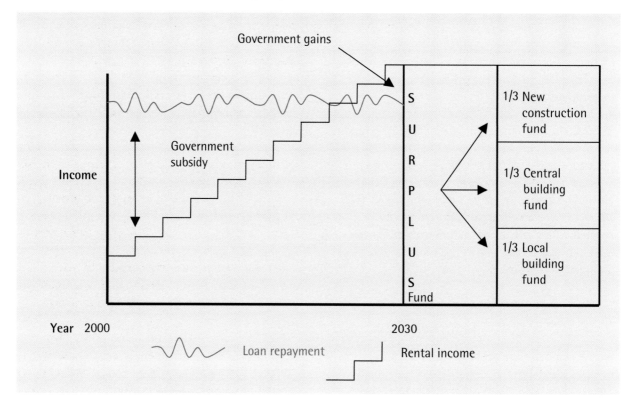

In Finland, subject to a minimum interest rate of 3.5%, the state pays half the interest costs for the first five years of the loan, 40% for years six to 10, and 30% until the loan is repaid at the end of the 18th year. (Although the government guarantee is restricted to the first 20 years of the loan, loans can be refinanced to increase maturity beyond the original term.)

The Swedish government restructured its interest subsidies in the 1990s, due to rising interest rates which caused their cost to rise six-fold between 1982 and 1992. Until 1992, construction was financed by a government loan, covering 20% of eligible costs, and a bank loan covering the remainder. The interest subsidy applied to the latter, with the interest rate pegged at 3.7%, and rising by 0.375% each year until the market rate was reached. The scheme now in operation in Sweden spreads the interest risk between the government and the social landlord. It is set at 30% for the duration of the loan to mimic the effect of tax relief in other tenures.

Other resources

Implicit subsidies are often delivered through the provision of cheap land, but are of course much more difficult to measure. Denmark is unique in

requiring tenants to make a contribution. This is set at 2% of development costs. Low income tenants can borrow the money from the municipality, or gain assistance from the housing allowance. Landlords also provide some of their own equity in a number of countries. Dutch housing associations provide an estimated 10% of the funds for finance. Using reserves became a feature of the English system when competitions for government grants were held, although running down reserves in this way is no longer encouraged for fear of undermining their capacity to carry out major repairs. In Germany and Finland, provision is made for an explicit rate of return to be made by social landlords on any equity which they themselves place in a development. This is set at 4% for investments of up to 15% in Germany and at 2 percentage points over government bonds in Finland.

Redistributing surpluses

When surpluses emerge in social rented housing there are four likely beneficiaries:

1. existing tenants, either through limiting the surplus through lower rents, or using the surplus to improve existing properties;

2. new tenants of the same landlord, as surpluses are used either to subsidise new construction or to subsidise rents on new houses (rent pooling);
3. tenants of other landlords, as surpluses are distributed from surplus landlords to deficit landlords; and
4. governments, which aim to recoup past subsidies.

Of course it is possible for surpluses to be shared between more than one beneficiary. Rent pooling and the extent to which tenants benefit from surpluses are described in more detail in Chapter 4, so here the experiences of governments recouping surpluses and of redistribution between landlords are examined.

Recouping surpluses by governments

Taken as a whole, English local authorities have been in surplus since the mid-1990s, but the recouping of these surpluses by the government through 'negative housing subsidy entitlement' (now exceeding £1 billion per year [Wilcox, 2000, table 65]) has been controversial due to the way the surpluses have been recouped through the Housing Benefit element of the subsidy. The replacement to this system implies the use of surpluses to fund major repairs through the establishment of a Major Repair Account. Some Swedish local authorities have attempted to recoup surpluses through sales programmes, with part of the receipt being returned to the local authority as the shareholder (see, for example, Svenska Bostäder (2000, p 38), where the transfer of funds to the municipality is described as 'distributed to shareholders' in the accounts).

Redistribution between landlords

As in England, there is a trend among Dutch housing associations towards mergers, often within a group structure. The extent to which mergers have occurred in England is somewhat difficult to demonstrate, as the figures are clouded by the large scale transfer of local authority housing to other registered social landlords. The figures available for the number of transfers of engagement do not distinguish between mergers and other forms of rationalisation. Similarly, in the first half of the 1990s it was difficult to demonstrate the extent to which mergers were

taking place in the Netherlands as any reduction in the number of housing associations due to merger was balanced by the transfer of the remainder of the municipal housing sector to the association sector. However, the number of housing associations in the Netherlands is clearly in decline and the average size of housing associations has increased rapidly (Priemus, 2001).

In both cases, mergers often combine associations with different financial profiles. In England, the process has in part been driven by the growing reliance of social landlords on private finance as smaller housing associations find it increasingly difficult to maintain a development role. The Housing Corporation sometimes facilitates mergers as a means of rescuing organisations in financial difficulty and maintaining the sector's record of 'no default' (Manley, 2000). The Dutch ministry of housing has also been particularly supportive of mergers between asset rich and asset poor associations. Merger may be further motivated in the Netherlands by a desire to avoid the compulsory redistribution of surpluses between associations.

Mergers are not always the ideal solution to redistributing surpluses. The process is not organised strategically at the level of the sector. Moreover, mergers often lack transparency and may be motivated by non-efficiency objectives, such as growth for growth's sake. The case of Denmark provides an example of a transparent mechanism for redistribution within the social rented sector. Although Denmark's social rented sector adheres to cost rental principles at the level of the estate, so in this respect is very fragmented, in terms of ownership structure it is comparatively cohesive. Cohesion arises from a single institutional model of social landlord, in contrast to Finland, or (especially) Germany.

Redistribution in the Danish system occurs at two levels:

1. *Local Building Fund:* Each housing association has its own building fund that can be used to redistribute funds between its estates in order to finance major repairs or renovations that cannot be funded by a particular estate.

2. *Central Building Fund:* This fund was established in 1967, originally to provide capital grants to subsidise new building. However, by the 1980s, it increasingly became used to finance renovations, particularly on 'problem' estates.

Each of these funds is supported by emerging rent surpluses as rents rise above debt repayments. Surpluses are divided between the two funds. Given the downward trend in new building, the amount of funds is predicted to grow very sharply. This has prompted the government to establish a third fund:

3. New Construction Fund – this fund is being established, in principle, to allow the sector to become self-reliant. It is intended that it should be used to subsidise new developments, which was, of course, the original purpose of the Central Building Fund. The fund will start receiving payments when new loans begin to be paid off in 2030. The other funds will continue to be supported by existing agreements. Surpluses will then be divided equally between the New Construction Fund and the other two funds.

The Danish example provides an example of how mechanisms can be established to attract rent surpluses. However, it should be noted that even in the Danish system, where the social rented sector consists of legally independent organisations, there are concerns that the funds might be vulnerable to being 'raided' by the government. In particular the New Construction Fund, although administered by the Central Building Fund, is controlled by the government. Moreover, there seems to be no mechanism for ensuring that surpluses are generated. Any adoption of a similar system would be likely to require some central direction over rent rises.

Summary

This chapter has described the ways in which social landlords are subsidised, and the following features were noted:

- Generally subsidies are aimed at lowering the cost of housing in the earlier years of the loan.

- For this reason, diminishing revenue or interest subsidy systems are frequently employed.

- Capital grants are less common, and play the most extensive role in Britain.

When surpluses arise:

- Governments sometimes attempt to recoup surpluses.

- Redistribution between landlords is very difficult to achieve in highly fragmented systems.

- Even in systems where social landlords are of a common type, a transparent system of redistribution is absent and landlords rely on ad hoc mergers.

- Denmark provides an example of a social rented sector with transparent mechanisms for redistributing surpluses.

Private finance for social rented housing

7

Introduction

The private sector is now the principal source of finance for construction in each of the countries surveyed, with the exception of French and Finnish state loan systems, and the British grant system.

The Dutch system is also now entirely dependent on private finance, except to the extent to which landlords can use their reserves to reduce the size of the loan. In 1995, under the 'grossing and balancing' operation, Dutch housing associations received a one-off payment from the government that was supposed to free associations from debt. To avoid breakage costs, associations retain debts on one side of their balance sheets, while retaining the one-off grant (invested) on the other. This exercise was intended to strengthen the housing associations' balance sheets sufficiently for the government to cease to subsidise the sector, which it has done. In Sweden, the total cost of development is also now met by private finance (subject to the subsidy regime outlined in Chapter 6). Danish social landlords raise 84% of their funds from the private market, the remaining funds being provided as a grant from the municipality.

Although the unusual British grant system means that housing associations and other registered social landlords in Britain are less dependent on private finance than their counterparts in several other European countries, it has become a vital part of the British system. This chapter examines in turn the sources and costs of private finance for social landlords.

Sources of private finance

Private finance is obtained mainly from the dominant kinds of banking intermediaries in the countries studied. For example, these are mortgage banks in Sweden and Denmark; in Britain banks and building societies; in Finland general banks. In Sweden and the Netherlands local government or state-owned intermediaries have been established to provide competition for the privately-owned lenders. SBAB is a state owned mortgage bank in Sweden whose function is to enhance competition and diversity in the mortgage market (SBAB, 2000).

As with the Housing Finance Corporation in Britain, an intermediary has been established in the Netherlands (in 1998) to access the capital markets on behalf of the housing associations. Collenade is owned by a non-profit foundation and is run by nominees of the housing associations and their representative body, AEDES. All its bonds are AAA rated.

English housing associations are unusual in that they also access the capital market directly to fund around 30% of conventional housing association development. More than two thirds of the 25 bonds issued by or on behalf of English housing associations since 1998 have received credit ratings. While three issues received top Aaa/AAA ratings (sometimes these were achieved through a monoline insurer), about half received ratings of Aa3/AA- (*Social Housing*, May 2001). These compare with bonds issued by Danish mortgage banks which are generally rated as AAA, AA+ or AA1, and the ratings for the Swedish bank SBAB's long-term debt of AA-/A1 (SBAB, 2000).

Securitisation

Although loans have been securitised in Sweden and Britain, by far the most extensive securitisation programme has been undertaken by the Finnish Housing Fund (ARA). A description of the institutional structure of the Housing Fund is given in the box in Chapter 6, p 34. Since 1995 the Housing Fund has securitised euro 2.3 billion of state loans in five issues (Table 9).

In these transactions the originator is the Housing Fund and special purpose vehicles (known as Fennica No 1, 2, etc), registered in Ireland for legal reasons, have been used. Collateral is provided by loans issued at least three years previously, with credit risk diversified by ensuring that the pool has a geographic spread of loans, and a variety of loan sizes. Risk is also reduced by taking loans with good payment records, loan-to-value ratios less than 95% at origination, and from areas with low vacancy rates. Credit enhancement is provided by a reserve fund of 1% of the value of the loan balances. The senior notes for Fennica No 5 were rated at Aaa by Moody's (Leonia Corporate Bank Credit Research, 2000). Importantly, the funds from securitisation do not score as public expenditure as the special purpose vehicles are the borrower, rather than the state, and there is no state guarantee on the securities issued. Moreover, the housing that is being financed is not state-owned. They have enabled the Housing Fund to maintain a programme of subsidised housing development without recourse to further public subsidy, with new state loans and interest subsidies financed almost entirely by loan repayments and securitisation.

The costs of private finance

Clearly, it is desirable for the costs of private finance to be minimised. In order to estimate the relative costs of private finance for social rented housing between countries, we cannot simply compare the interest rate on the loans in these countries. This is because general interest rates (those set by central banks) can vary greatly between countries. For members of the euro, a single interest rate is now set by the European Central Bank, so aiding transparency between members. But Britain, Sweden and Denmark are not members of the single currency.

Instead, we have collected information on interest rate margins (or spreads). These measure the difference between the actual interest rate on a loan and a benchmark rate, which is supposed to represent the minimum cost of borrowing money for a similar term or interest rate structure. Other things being equal, the smaller the margin, the cheaper the finance. For fixed interest rate loans, the most appropriate benchmark for measuring the efficiency of the system is the appropriate government bond rate, since this measures the cost of fixed rate risk-free borrowing (on the basis that governments do not default because they can raise taxes).

The most common substitute benchmark rate is the inter-bank offer rate, which is the rate at which banks lend money to one another. This is often used for measuring the margin on variable rate loans. Sometimes, appropriate central bank base rates are also used.

In principle, the margin reflects three influences, which are difficult to distinguish between:

- the risk of lending to a social landlord, likely to be affected by factors such as the financial strength and managerial competence of individual housing associations;
- the presence of sector-wide safeguards, such as guarantees; and
- the degree of efficiency and competition among lenders.

Table 9: Transactions in the Fennica Programme 1995–2000

Fennica number	Issued	Original amount	Issue currency	Amount in EUR (m.)[a]
1	1995	363.7	USD	412.5
2	1996	1,507.0	FIM	253.5
3	1998	2,052.0	FIM[b]	345.1
4	1999	500.0	EUR	500.0
5	2000	800.0	EUR	800.0
Total				2,311.1

Notes:
[a] EURUSD = 0.8818 (6/9/00); EURFIM = 5.94573
[b] Converted to euros in 1999
Sources: ARA; Ministry of the Environment

In practice margin analysis is vulnerable to other influences, including the effects of interest rate cycles. They can vary on a year to year basis. Margins can also be affected by the way in which arrangement costs are charged. For example, some costs may take the form of a separate charge or they may simply influence the interest rate. Moreover, the terms attached to loans are also likely to affect margins. For example, those that permit prepayment without penalty are more likely to have wider margins than those that do not. It was not possible to consider these factors in this survey. Consequently, the results should be treated as indicative.

Table 10 presents evidence of margins from six countries (counting England and Scotland separately). It also indicates where guarantees exist and gives estimates of their impact on margins. While treating the results with caution, the table indicates that:

Table 10: The cost of private finance

	Spread (basis points)	Benchmark rate	Cost of guarantee to landlord	Estimated value of guarantee (bp)
Denmark	20-30	GB	0	20
Finland	30-40	IBOR	0	-
The Netherlands	20-40	GB	- initial membership fee - commission - set aside 2.5-3.75%[a]	100
Sweden				
strong	20-25			
weak	100	GB	0	20
securitisation	40			
England				
VR LIBOR[b]	53.4	IBOR		
FR <7 yrs[c]	164	5 yr GB		
FR 7-16 yrs[d]	180	10 yr GB	na	na
FR > 20 yrs[e]	170	20 yr GB		
Bond issues 1998-2001[f]	126.4	GB		
Scotland[g]				
VR 1999[h]	113.8 (a) 81.2			
VR 2000[i]	84.0	BR	na	na
FR 1999[k]	113.8			
FR 2000[l]	325.9			

Key: GB = government bond; IBOR = inter-bank offered rate; na = not applicable; VR = variable rate; FR = fixed rate; BR = base rate
Notes:
[a] Housing associations are required to make these sums available should the capital available to WSW fall below 0.25% of guarantees extended.
[b] Figure given as 0.534% by NHF = weighted average for FYE 1999
[c] Figure given by NHF less average 5 year government security Q3, 1998-Q1, 1999
[d] Figure given by NHF less average 10 year government security Q3, 1998-Q1, 1999
[e] Figure given by NHF less average 20 year government security Q3, 1998-Q1, 1999
[f] Weighted average of 25 bond issues 1998-2001 listed in *Social Housing* (range = 75-204), May 2001. *Social Housing* uses interest rate less various Treasury securities to calculate margin.
[g] Loans for new build. Calculated from information provided by Scottish Homes
[h] Range = 25-321
[i] Range = 55-184
[k] Range = 70-323
[l] Range = 131-410
Source: Finland: ARA; Sweden: SBAB, except securisitation = Svenska Bostäder; England: NHF Private Finance Loans Bulletin 2000, except bond issues = *Social Housing* and interest rates = Bank of England *Monetary and Financial Statistics;* Scotland: Scottish Homes

- The cost of funds appears to be significantly higher in England and Scotland than in the three other countries.
- The range in margins also seems to be much greater in England and Scotland than elsewhere.
- In England and Scotland, where there is a much stronger tradition of variable rate lending, the margins on variable rate loans appear to be smaller than on fixed rate loans and on bond issues. The higher cost of fixed rate borrowing is at least partly attributable to hedging costs, while a different benchmark is used for bonds.

An analysis of the impact of the credit rating of bond issues on margins in England (Table 11) shows that the margin on bond issues is not wholly consistent with credit ratings received. For example the average margin (weighted for the size of issue) on the 12 issues rated Aa3/AA- are much higher than the eight that were not rated.

The explanation for this counter-intuitive finding appears to be that margins on all bonds rose considerably in 1998 and 1999, and remained well above their 1998 level in 2001 (Table 12). Since

Table 11: Margins on bond issues according to credit ratings

Credit rating	Number of bond issues	Weighted margin (bp)
None	8	108.6
Aaa/AAA	3	98.2
Aa3/AA-	12	146.6
Other	2	88
All	25	126.4

Source: Calculated from *Social Housing*

Table 12: Margins on bond issues by year

Year	Number of bond issues	Weighted margin (bp)
1998	13	92.8
1999	5	147.4
2000	5	188.5
2001	2	138.5
All	25	126.4

Source: Calculated from *Social Housing*

more recent bond issues have been more likely to be credit rated, it would appear that any benefit of credit rating has been outweighed by the general rise in margins.

The role of guarantees

The margins paid by British housing associations/ registered social landlords do appear to be much higher than elsewhere. While the estimates of margins in this report are higher than in some other studies, even these appear to suggest that British social landlords pay more for their money[1].

Although the British housing association/ registered social landlord sector has a number of strengths, such as a strong regulatory system and the support given to the income stream by Housing Benefit, a number of factors may contribute to the apparently high cost of finance in Britain. Some of these factors have worsened in recent years. These include:

- a narrow and narrowing social base;
- political risk associated with the high dependence on Housing Benefit to pay rents;
- reduced flexibility over rent setting (due to the Housing Corporation's control over rent rises);
- increased indebtedness of the sector;
- low demand in some areas;
- lack of power of regulators to force mergers; and
- no formal guarantee[2].

Britain is not alone in shifting more risk from government to social landlords, the changes in the Swedish subsidy system being a prime case, and there may be many reasons why margins may appear to be so much wider in Britain than elsewhere. These will fall into two categories:

- problems of measurement relating to interest cycles and so on, which may mean that margins in Britain are not permanently higher than elsewhere; and

---

[1] Whitehead (1999) reported margins (over LIBOR) of 200 basis points when English housing associations first began to access private finance, falling to somewhere in the range of 50–75 basis points.

[2] These issues are noted and discussed in Manley (2000).

The role of the guarantee fund in the Dutch housing system

The Dutch guarantee fund (*Waarborgfonds Sociale Woningbouw* – WSW) was established in 1983 by the housing associations' representative organisations, but was capitalised by the government. Membership of the guarantee fund is voluntary, and subject to each member passing a test of financial strength, and the payment of a membership fee. However, 90% of housing associations are members of WSW. Membership does not ensure that each loan can be guaranteed. WSW performs an important regulatory role in the Dutch social housing system, and carries out annual financial monitoring reports on each association. Each loan must be approved by WSW and is subject to a commission. Subject to these provisos, loans taken out for new build, property acquisition, renovation and refinancing may be guaranteed. Should an association cease to meet WSW's financial criteria, existing loans remain guaranteed, but no new ones will be guaranteed until the financial criteria are met. In addition to the membership fee and commission, members are obliged to set aside 2.5–3.75% of the original amount insured which may be called on should WSW's capital fall below 0.25%. Should the housing associations be unable to pay, then the government and municipalities share equal responsibility for providing unlimited funds, which would take the form of interest-free loans to WSW.

It is important to note that WSW is one institutional element within the Dutch housing system that contributes to the sector's ability to raise finance at low margins (see Diagram 3):

- *Grossing and balancing exercise:* As the government pursued its objective of reducing its role in housing policy, it reached an agreement with the housing associations, whereby the associations would be relieved of their debt, while the government would be relieved of future subsidy obligations from 1 January 1995. The exercise is sometimes presented as a debt write-off. In reality, the debts remain on the housing association balance sheets, but the government paid the present value of future subsidies to the associations. In this way expensive breakage costs were avoided.

- *The Central Housing Fund:* A second source of financial support is provided by the Central Housing Fund (CFV), which was established by the government in 1987. The fund exists to assist associations which encounter difficulties, whether or not they are members of WSW. It is funded through compulsory contributions from the housing associations and financial support normally takes the form of interest-free loans. Financial support is conditional on implementation of a rescue plan. CFV may work with WSW during a rescue. To date 15 associations have been helped in this way.

Diagram 3: The Dutch social housing system

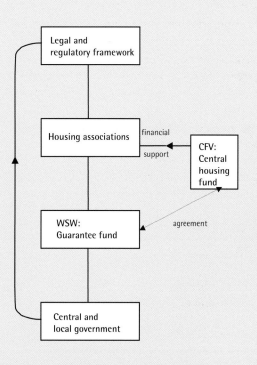

Source: adapted from WSW

- unidentified structural features, for example relating to the structure of the sector, the conditions attached to loans, and the level of competition between lenders.

A much more detailed study of margins would be required to reach firm conclusions, but one distinctive feature of the British system is the absence of a system of guarantees (although some Swedish municipalities are phasing out guarantees; see Sheridan et al, 2000), and this provides a likely explanation for at least some of the difference in costs. The way in which the Dutch government has created an institutional structure, including a guarantee system, to support a financially independent housing association sector is instructive. A description of the role of the Dutch guarantee fund within the social housing system is contained in the box overleaf.

The Dutch guarantee fund (WSW) estimates that the guarantee shaves up to one percentage point off the cost of funds for housing associations and reduces rents by 5–10%. However, the following caveats should be noted:

- The benefits of membership of WSW are likely to be uneven reflecting the heterogeneous composition of the membership. The effect of the guarantee may be to lower the cost of funds for the smaller housing associations and to allow them to maintain their capacity for development. It is notable that mergers tend to occur between (larger) associations of similar sizes, rather than between small and large associations. (For this reason some English housing associations have formed intermediaries, believing that their financial strength would gain lower prices than if they used the Housing Financial Corporation.)
- It is difficult to isolate the benefits of the guarantee, from the benefits of regulation by WSW, the Central Housing Fund (CFV) and the favourable financial legacy bequeathed to the associations following the balancing and grossing exercise.
- WSW has received credit ratings of Aaa by Moody's. Although Aaa ratings have been achieved on some bond issues by English housing associations, the cost of funds to them nevertheless exceeds the cost to Dutch housing associations.

- The government and the municipalities act as 'catchers' (that is, ultimate guarantors) and this has given rise to some concern that the sector might be drawn within the European Commission's definition of public expenditure.
- Despite the guarantee structure, funds remain more expensive than funds raised by central and local government. WSW has been unable to find a reason for this.

Summary

From a British perspective, the main findings of this review of private finance are:

- Due to the British system of capital grants, registered social landlords/housing associations are less dependent on private finance than their counterparts in the countries surveyed.

- Nevertheless, private finance in Britain appears to be more expensive than in other countries, and its cost seems to vary more between landlords.

- A much more detailed study is required to identify the reasons for these differences.

- However, the absence of a guarantee in Britain seems likely to contribute to the higher costs of funds.

8

Conclusions

This report has examined a wide range of policies relating to social rented housing in Britain and six other European countries. Moreover, housing policies have been placed within the social and economic context in which they have been developed. Detailed summaries relating to the aspects of policy are given at the end of the relevant chapters and are not repeated here.

From the preceding analysis and conclusions it is possible to draw three main conclusions.

1. British social housing operates in a quite different social and economic context from the other countries studied

Britain has generally greater levels of poverty and income inequality than in the other countries studied. Earnings are more dispersed and work is distributed more unequally in Britain. These are not corrected by the tax and benefits system to the extent that they are in other countries. Consequently, the social rented sector in Britain plays more of a safety net role than in the other countries where it contributes to enhancing the affordability of housing for a wider range of income groups.

2. The priority given to social rented housing in providing a safety net makes it difficult to create a social market within it

Tenants in British social rented housing are very poor. Given their circumstances and incomes, it is very difficult for them to exercise market or market-type choices. Where they do they are likely to do so from a weak position in relation to others. This conclusion is particularly relevant to

proposals for reforming allocation systems, rent structures and Housing Benefit.

3. Consequently, the priority in British housing policy should be to ensure that the social rented sector provides a comprehensive and high quality safety net

Housing policy must be formulated within the social and economic context in which it operates. This does not preclude the possibility of that social and economic context changing over time, but for the foreseeable future the priority accorded to the safety net function is necessary.

More detailed recommendations follow from these conclusions. They have been informed by the study of institutional features of the housing systems in the countries studied.

1. The role of the social rented sector should be defined by the government. In order to ensure a long-term stable environment, it is desirable that these objectives should be broadly based and command widespread political consensus. The sector should be accountable and be regulated, both in relation to the fulfilment of obligations and operational efficiency. However, it is desirable that the sector should be insulated from short-term political interference, in order to ensure a stable financial framework and encourage long-term planning, particularly relating to maintenance.

2. Allocations policy should be directed at providing a guarantee of housing for homeless and other vulnerable groups. Moreover, allocation systems should be designed to ensure that they do not weaken the choices of the most vulnerable applicants relative to

others. Need should remain the principal criterion for allocation in order to ensure that the safety net role is fulfilled. More limited offers, 'time cards' and other mechanisms that weaken the position of vulnerable households should be avoided in order to minimise polarisation within the sector.

3. Social rented housing can be provided by a variety of institutional types, such as housing associations and municipal housing companies. Differences in governance structure (for example the extent of tenant involvement) may also be appropriate according to size and other factors. Local monopolies should be avoided to ensure that tenants' interests are protected.

4. Two landlord types should be avoided. First, private landlords seem an inappropriate vehicle for the provision of social rented housing in Britain. They are best suited to meeting housing shortages, rather than providing a solution to enduring affordability problems and safety net priorities. Second, housing directly owned and managed by local government sits uneasily within this model. The short political cycle sits uneasily beside the need to create a culture of long-term planning into British rented housing.

5. Social landlords should operate within a common legal, financial and regulatory regime. It is important that solidarity exists in the sector, rather than short-term institutional competition or empire building. Just as commitments to housing the most vulnerable groups should be shared, so the same subsidies should be available between landlords, and the same expectations of performance should prevail.

6. A rent surplus fund for the sector as a whole should be established. Rental surpluses should be protected from 'raids' by the government, but under the principle of solidarity they should not be seen as the property of any one landlord. Once the maintenance requirements of a landlord are fulfilled, surpluses should be placed in a fund that would redistribute funds between landlords in order to meet three objectives: (i) to facilitate common rent policies, (ii) to provide funds for long-term maintenance for financially weak landlords, and (iii) to provide funds for development.

The fund would provide a significantly more transparent means of redistribution between landlords than is provided by mergers and would enhance the survival prospects of smaller landlords. Such a fund, under the control of the sector as a whole could be developed learning from the Danish experience.

7. Common pricing structures between landlords are desirable. For our purposes they would be necessary in order to ensure that landlords with rental surpluses do not simply restrain rents and fail to contribute to the rent surplus fund. Rent rises should be agreed annually by representatives of the fund, the sector, government and tenants. Common rent structures are desirable to ensure equity between tenants, but the benefits of this would be limited by the high proportion of tenants who receive Housing Benefit.

8. Housing Benefit should continue to meet the whole rent of tenants living in social rented housing who are in receipt of social assistance benefits. Without long-term benefit reform, the extent to which meaningful shopping incentives can be introduced is limited, even when social assistance levels are enhanced to include an allowance for housing. If the objective of Housing Benefit were broadened to extend its affordability function, a dual taper system would introduce shopping incentives for tenants better able to exercise market choices.

9. The case for a guarantee fund based on the Dutch model should be considered. This report suggested that the cost of private finance to British social landlords is somewhat higher than in other European countries. A much more detailed study is required before firm conclusions can be reached.

10. Policy should be reviewed in (say) ten years' time. It is possible that labour market and social security reforms will have created more favourable conditions for the broadening of the function of the social rented sector and the movement away from a safety net and towards a social market.

References

ARA (Housing Fund of Finland) (2000) *Social housing – pride of the nation*, Helsinki: ARA.

Blanc, M. (1998) 'Social integration and exclusion in France: some introductory remarks from a social transaction perspective', *Housing Studies*, vol 13, no 6, pp 781–92.

Borresen, S.K. (1996) 'The ethnic aspect of socio-economic segregation in the housing market', paper presented at European Network for Housing Research Conference, 'Housing and European Integration', Helsingør, Denmark, August 26–31.

DETR (Department of the Environment, Transport and the Regions) (2000a) *Quality and choice: A decent home for all, The way forward for housing*, London: DETR/DSS.

DETR (2000b) *Arms length management of local authority housing: a consultation paper*, London: DETR.

DETR (2000c) *Quality and choice: A decent home for all*, The Housing Green Paper, London: DETR

DETR (2001a) Choice-based lettings newsletter, issue 1, June.

DETR (2001b) *A guide to social rent reforms*, London: DETR.

DoE/DETR (Department of the Environment/ Department of the Environment, Transport and the Regions) *Housing and construction statistics*, Various issues, London: HMSO/The Stationery Office.

Dickens, R. Gregg, P. and Wadsworth, J. (2001) 'Non-working classes: Britain's new chronic unemployment', *CentrePiece*, vol 8, no 2, pp 11–19.

Doling, J (1997) *Comparative housing policy: Government and housing in advanced industrialized countries*, Basingstoke: Macmillan.

ECB (European Central Bank) (2000) *Annual Report 1999*, ECB: Frankfurt am Mein.

EMI (European Monetary Institute) (1998) *Convergence report*, EMI: Frankfurt am Mein.

European Commission (1998) *Social protection in Europe 1997*, Luxembourg: Office of Official Publications for the European Community.

Fitzpatrick, S. and Stephens, M. (1999) 'Homelessness, need and desert in the allocation of council housing', *Housing Studies*, vol 18, no 4, pp 413–31.

Gregg, P. and Wadsworth, J. (1996) 'It takes two: employment polarisation in the OECD', Centre for Economic Performance (CEP) Discussion Paper no 34, London: CEP.

Hills, J. (1991) *Unravelling housing finance: Subsidies, benefits, and taxation*, Oxford: Clarendon Press.

Kemp, P. (1997) *A comparative study of housing allowances*, London: The Stationery Office.

Kemp, P. (1998) 'Housing Benefit: Time for reform', *Findings*, no 178, York: Joseph Rowntree Foundation.

Kemp, P. (2000) 'The role and design of income-related housing allowances', *International Social Security Review*, vol 53, no, 3, pp 43–57.

Kullberg, J (1997) 'From waiting lists to adverts: The allocation of social rental dwellings in the Netherlands', *Housing Studies*, vol 12, no 3, pp 393–403.

Lakin, C (2001) 'The effects of taxes and benefits on household income, 1999–2000', *Economic Trends*, April, pp 35–74.

Leonia Corporate Bank Credit Research (2000) 'Fennica no 5: Securitisation of Finnish State Housing Loans', 18 September.

McCrone, G. and Stephens, M. (1995) *Housing policy in Britain and Europe*, London: UCL Press.

Manley, J. (2000) 'Broomleigh Housing Association', in Standard & Poor (eds) *Rating social and public housing provider's: A changing universe*, November, New York, NY: Standard & Poor's.

Moody's Investment Services (1999) *Waarborgfonds Sociale Woningbouw*, New York: Moody's.

OECD (Organisation for Economic Co-operation and Development) (1998a) *The battle against exclusion: Social assistance in Belgium, the Czech Republic, the Netherlands and Norway*, Paris: OECD.

OECD (1998b) *The battle against exclusion: Social assistance in Australia, Finland, Sweden and the United Kingdom*, Paris: OECD.

OECD (1998c) *Benefit systems and work incentives*, Paris: OECD.

OECD (1999) *Economic surveys. Denmark 1999*, Paris: OECD.

Oxley, M. and Smith, J. (1996) *Housing policy and rented housing in Europe*, London: E&FN Spon.

Pawson, H. and Kintrea, K. (2002) 'Part of the problem or part of the solution? Social housing allocation policies and social exclusion in Britain', *Journal of Social Policy*, forthcoming.

Power, A. (1993) *Hovels to high rise: State housing in Europe since 1850*, London: Routledge.

Priemus, H. (2001) 'Social housing as a transitional tenure? Reflections on the Netherlands' New Housing Memorandum 2000–2010', *Housing Studies*, vol 16, no 2, pp 243–56.

Remkes, J.W. (2000) 'Nota Wonen (Ontwerp) Mensen, Wensen, Wonen. Wonen in de 21e Eeuw' (Draft Housing Memorandum. People, Preferences, Housing. Housing in the 21st Century), The Hague: VROM. (Translation provided by WSW).

Scottish Executive (2000) *Better homes for Scotland's communities: The Executive's proposals for the Housing Bill*, Edinburgh; Scottish Executive.

Sheridan, T.J., Manley, J., MacDonald, C., Sars, A. and Flyn, B. (2000) 'Sliding scale of support: government role in housing' in Standard & Poor's (eds) (2000) *Rating social and public housing providers: a changing universe*, November, New York, NY: Standard & Poor's.

Skifter Anderson, H. (1999) *Self perpetuating processes of deprivation in 500 Danish social housing estates*, Horshølm: Danish Building Research Institute (SBI).

Social Housing, various issues.

Standard & Poor's (eds) (2000) *Rating social and public housing providers: A changing universe*, November, New York, NY: Standard & Poor's.

Stephens, M. (1998) 'Fiscal restraint and housing policies under economic and monetary union' in M. Kleinman, W. Matznetter, and M. Stephens (eds) *European integration and housing policy*, London: Routledge.

Stephens, M. (1999) 'The fiscal role of the European Union: The case of housing and the European structural funds', *Urban Studies*, vol 36, no 4, pp 715–35.

SBAB (2000) *Annual Report 1999*, Stockholm: SBAB.

Svenska Bostäder (2000) *Annual Report 1999*, Stockholm: Svenska Bostäder.

United Nations Centre for Human Settlements (HABITAT) (2001) *Cities in a globalizing world: Global report on human settlements 2001*, London and Sterling, VA: Earthscan.

Vogel, J (1997) *Living conditions and inequality in the European Union*, Eurostat Working Papers E/1997–3.

Walker, R (1998) 'Regulatory and organizational issues in market-led social housing: the case of the Netherlands', *Regional Studies*, vol 32, no 1, pp 79–84.

Whitehead, C.M.E. (1999) 'The provision of finance for social housing: the UK experience', *Urban Studies*, vol 36, no 4, pp 657–82.

Wilcox, S. (1998) *Unfinished business: Housing costs and the reform of housing benefits*, Coventry: Chartered Institute of Housing.

Wilcox, S. (2000) *Housing Finance Review 2000/ 2001*, Coventry/London: Chartered Institute of Housing/Council of Mortgage Lenders.